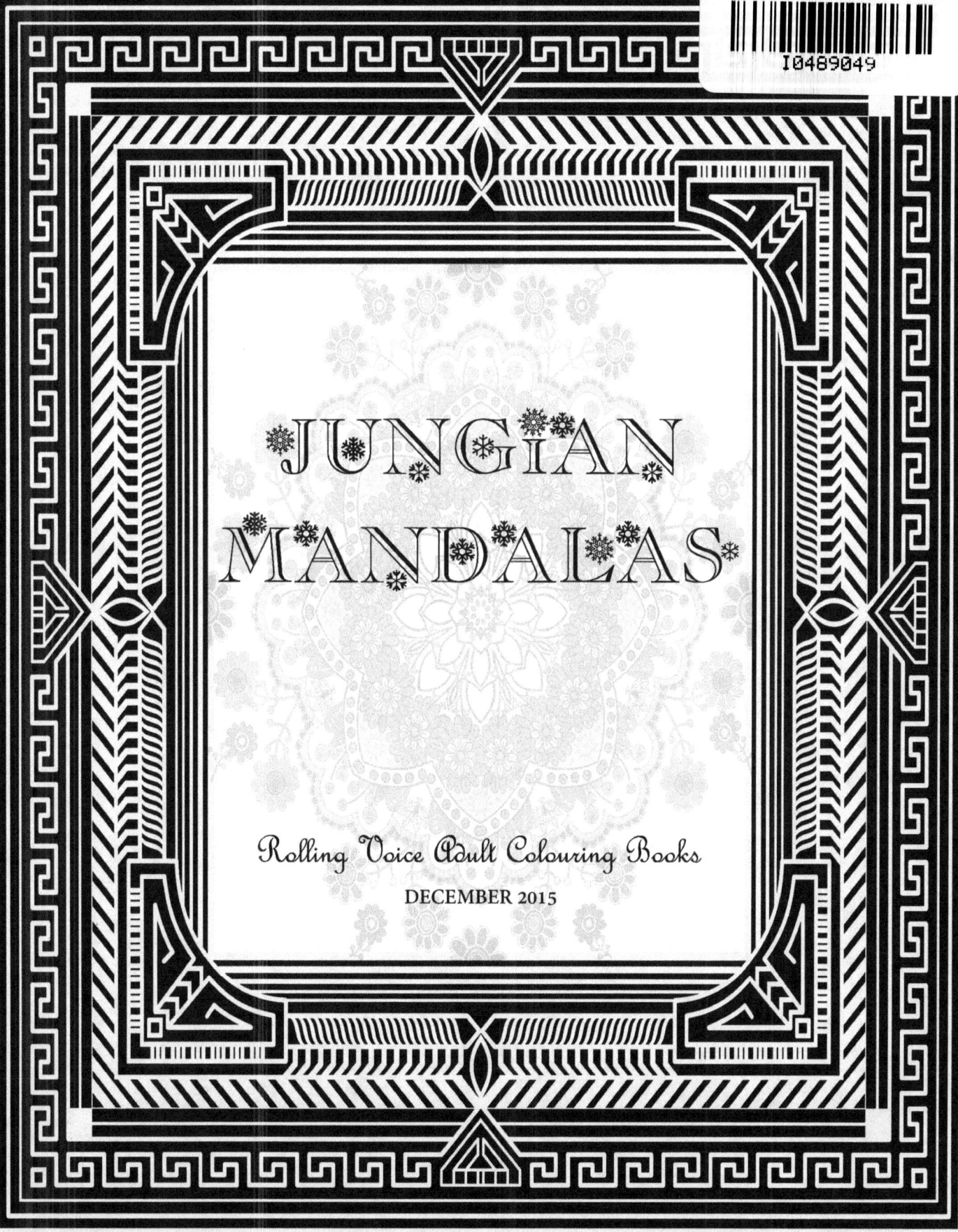

JUNGIAN MANDALAS

Rolling Voice Adult Colouring Books

DECEMBER 2015

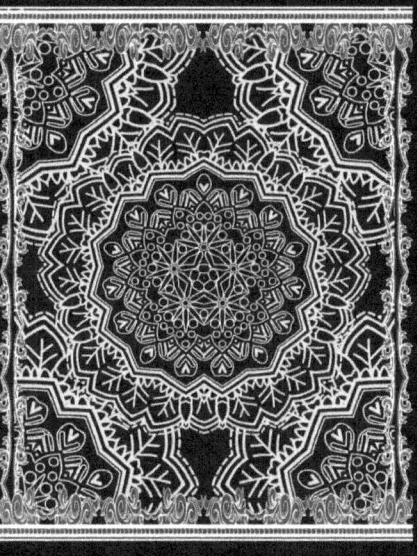
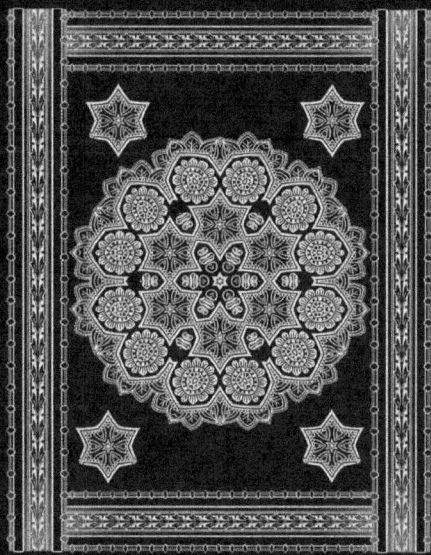
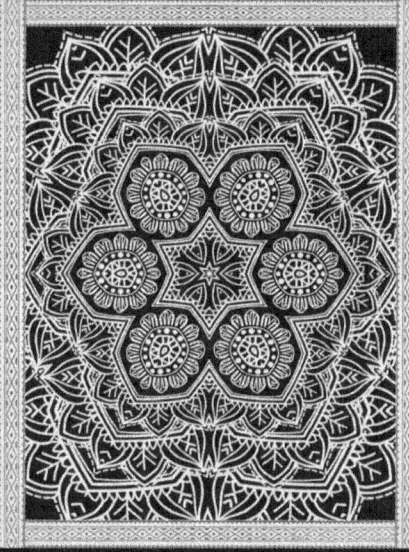

PREVIEWS

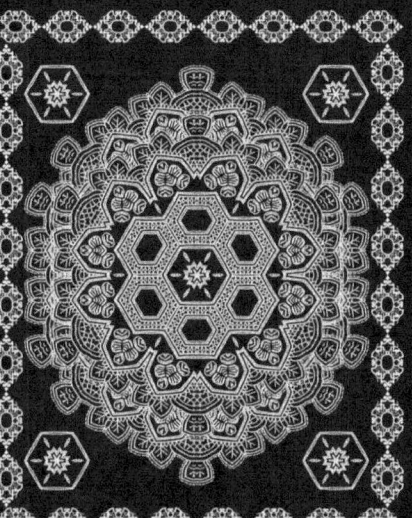
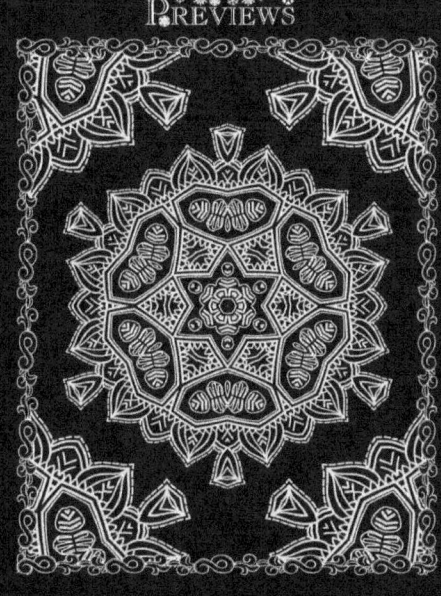
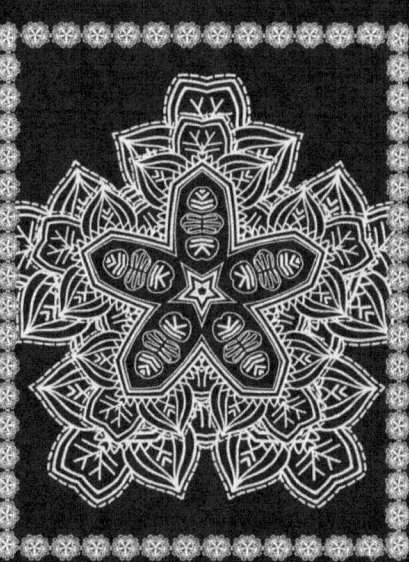

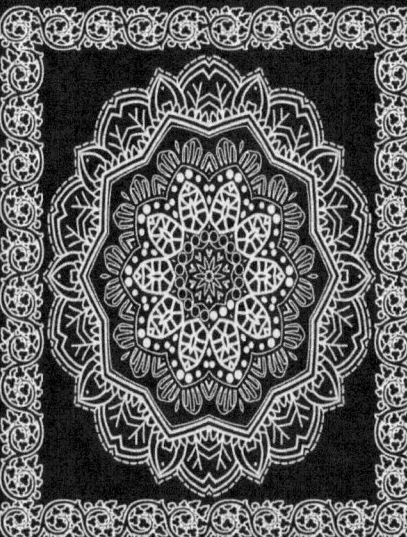
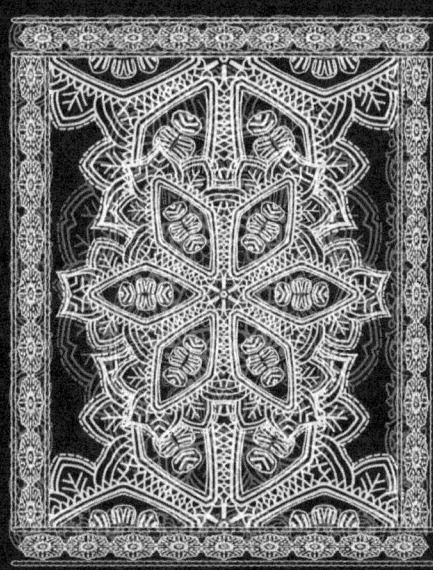
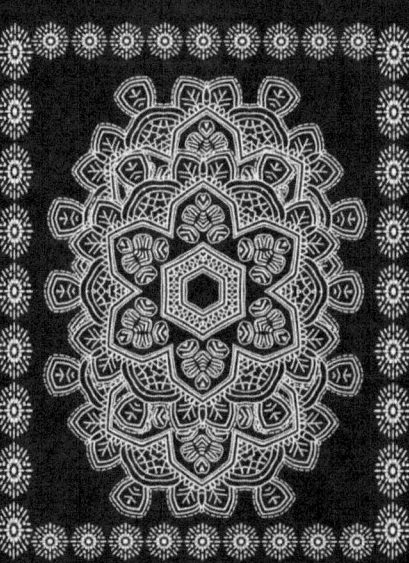

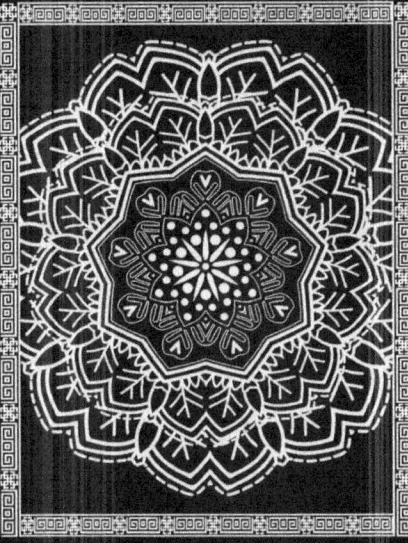
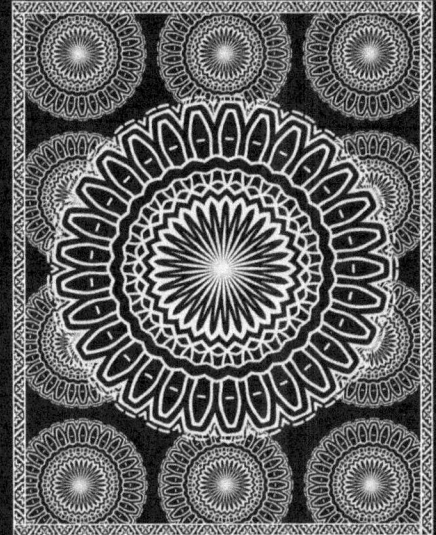
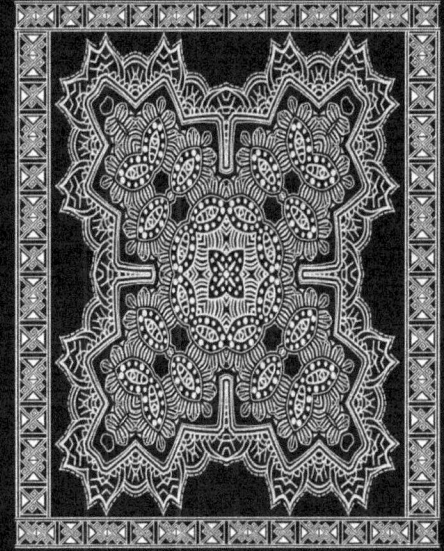

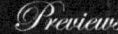

Previews

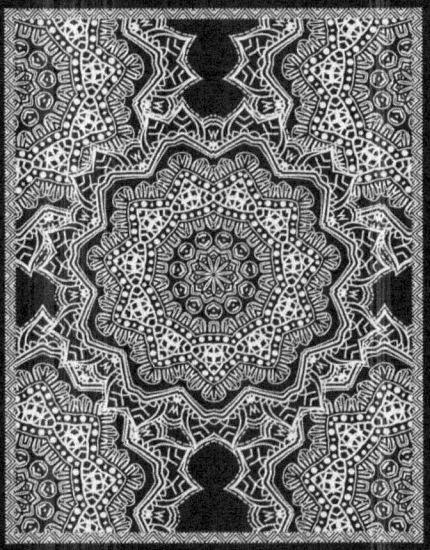
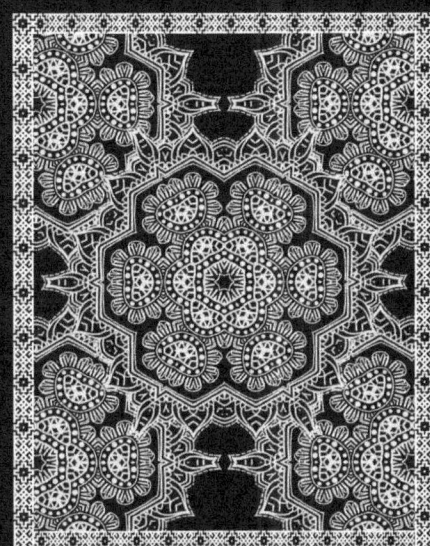
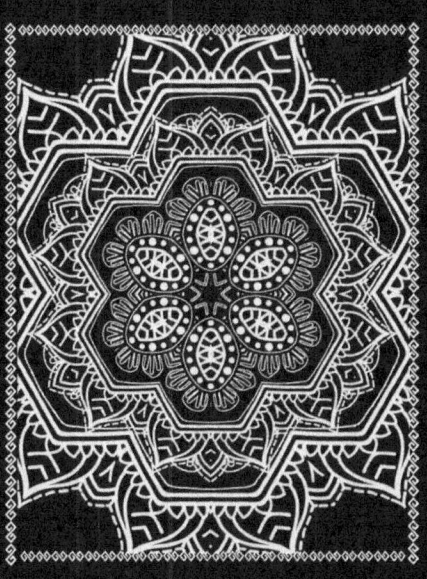

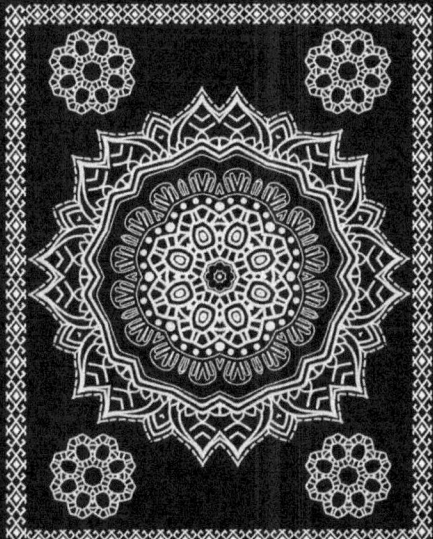
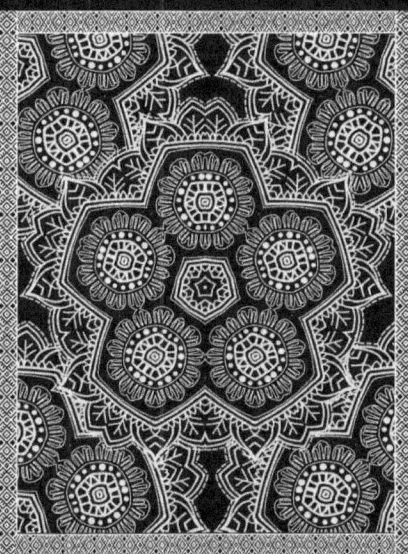

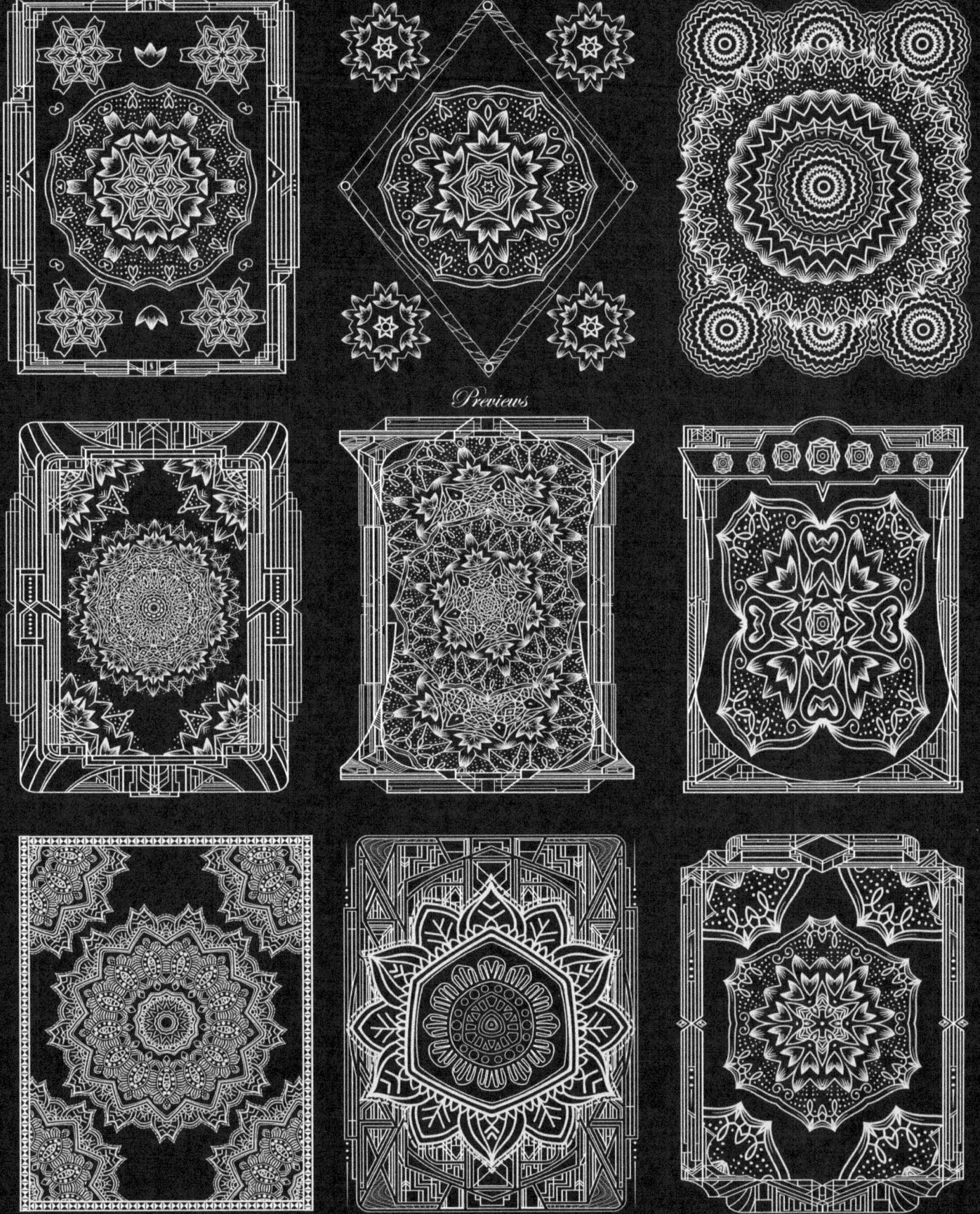

Previews

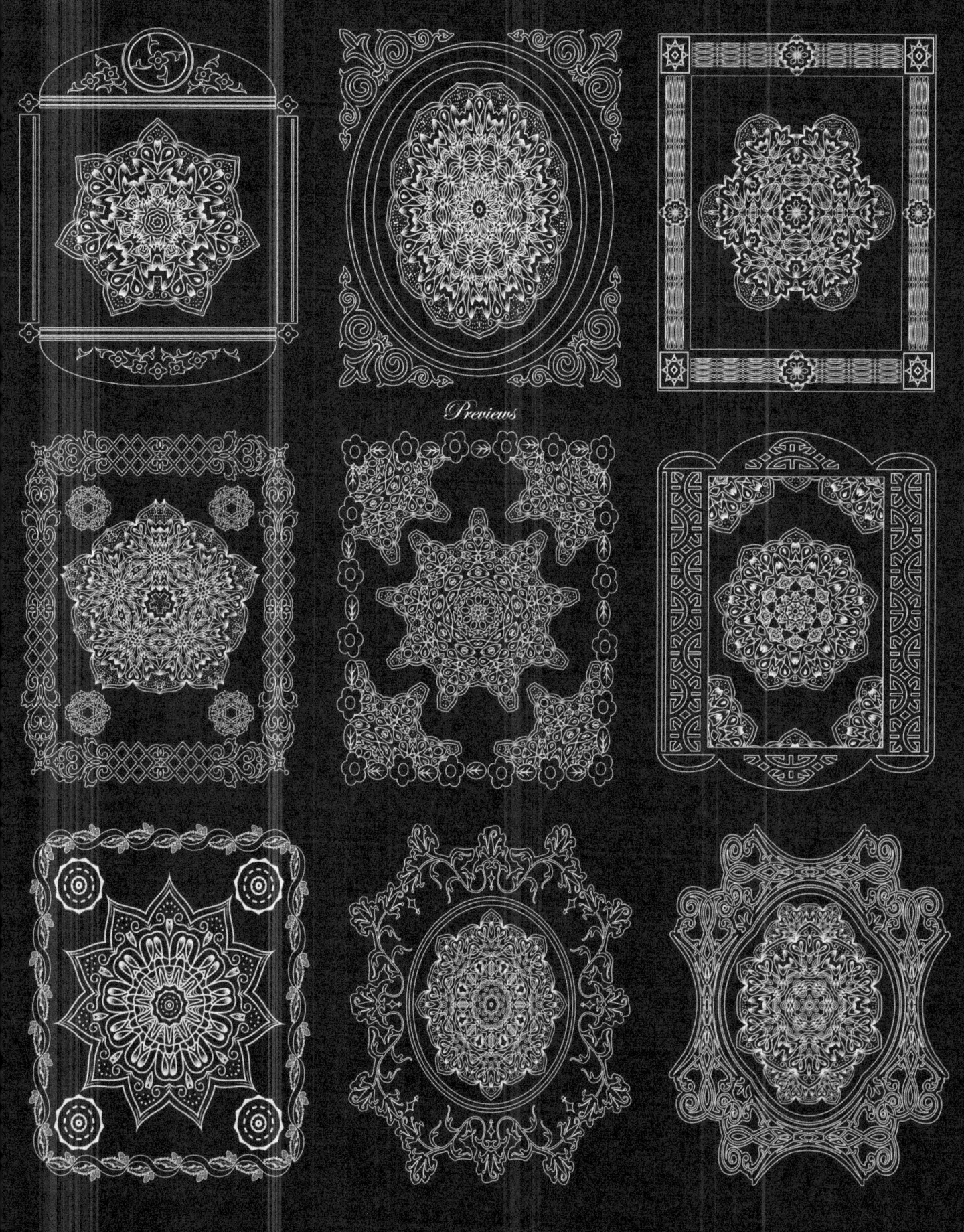

Previews

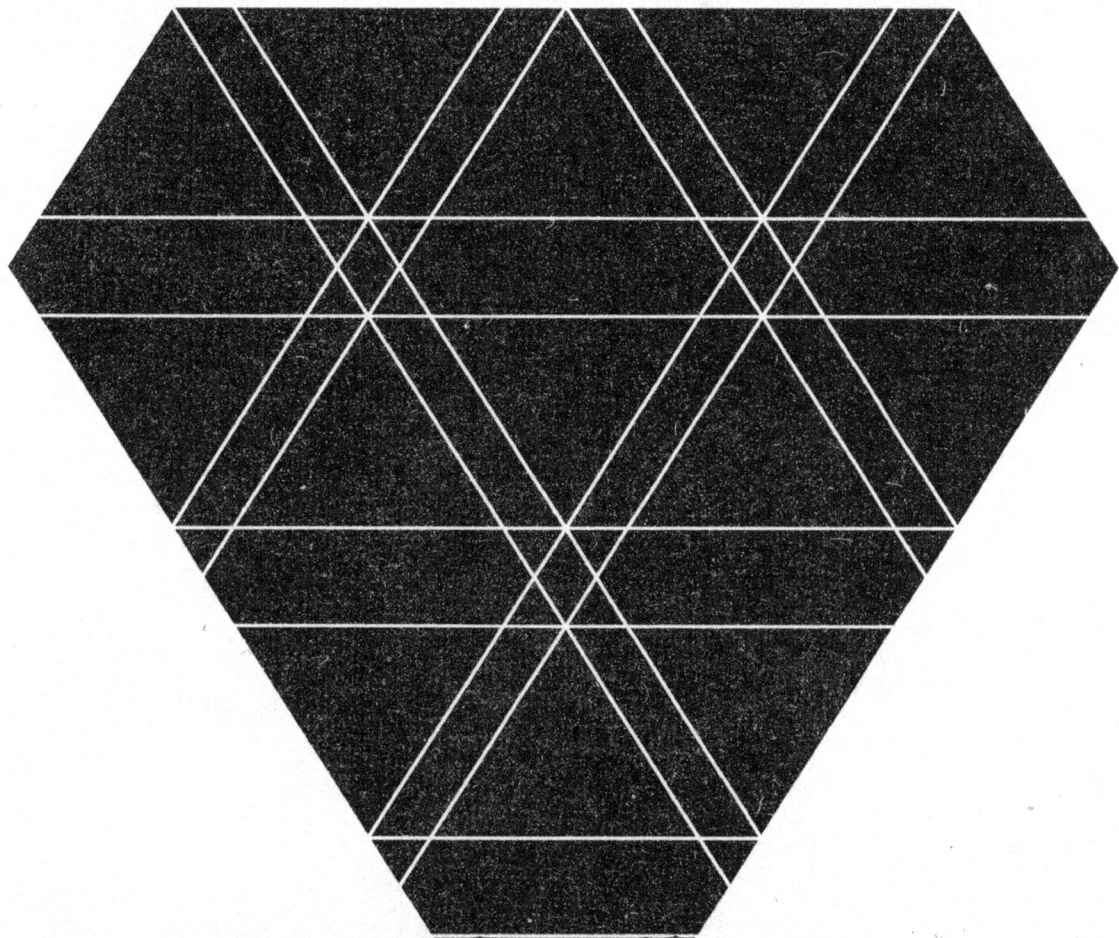

Printed in the United States of America

First Printing, 2015

ISBN-13: 978-1519328281

ISBN-10: 1519328281

Rolling Voice Publishing
33 Lower Park, Chartfield Avenue
London, UK SW15 6QY

www.RollingVoice.com

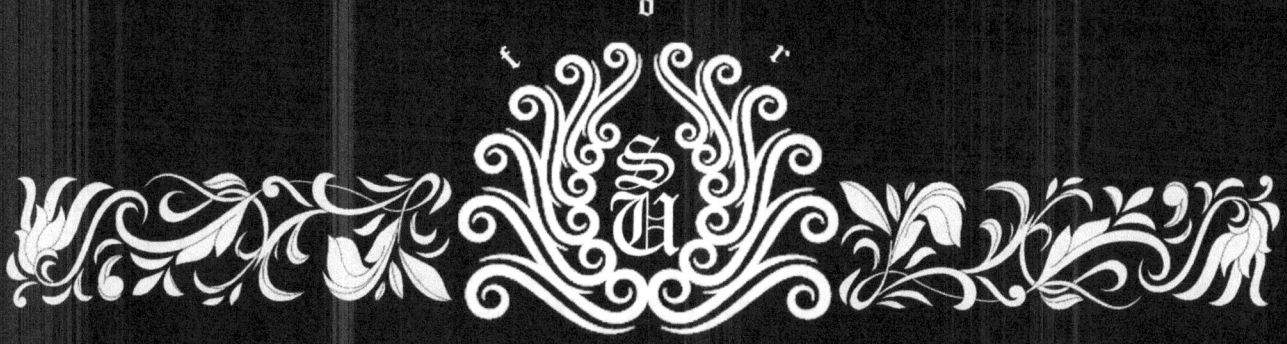

for

s
u

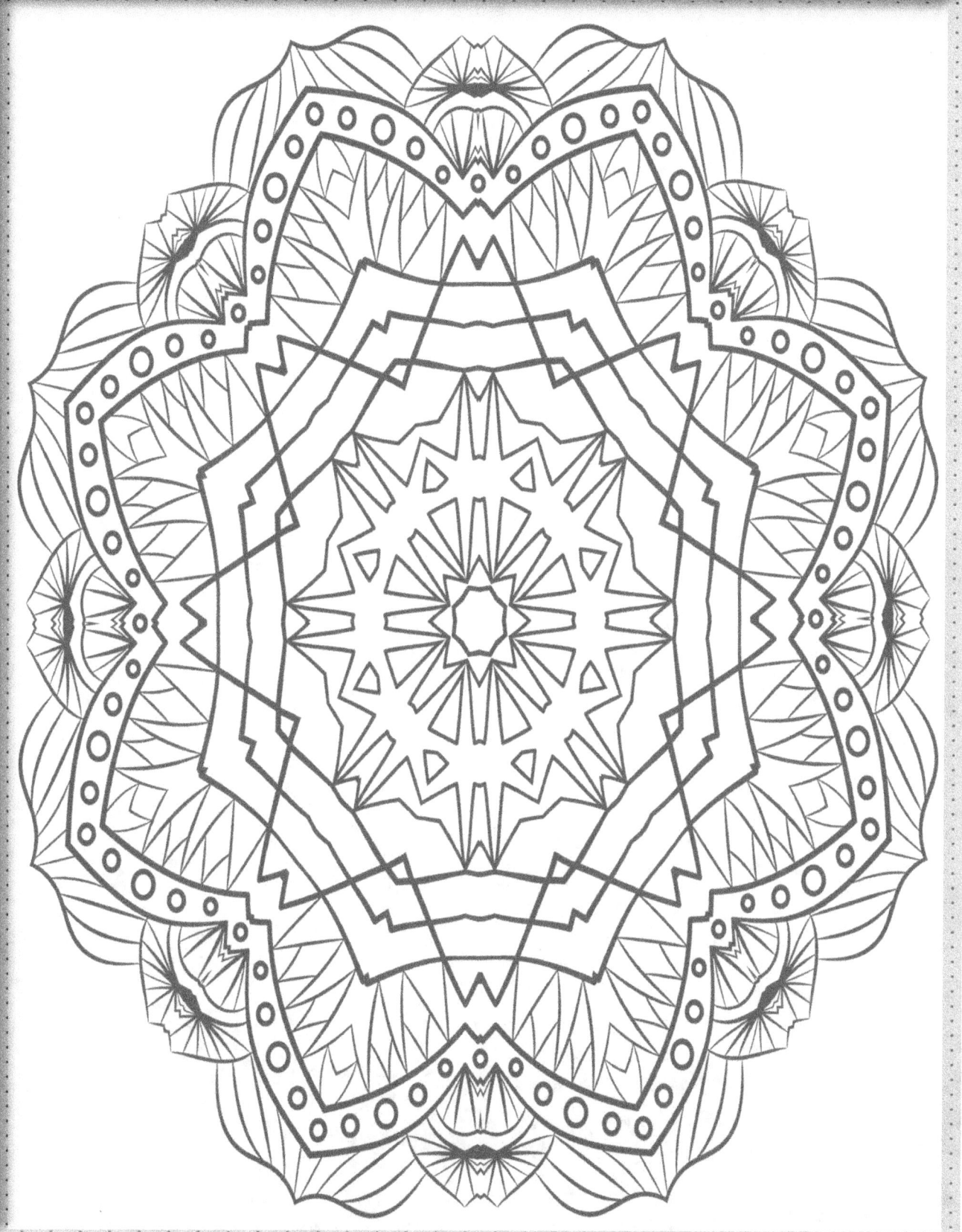

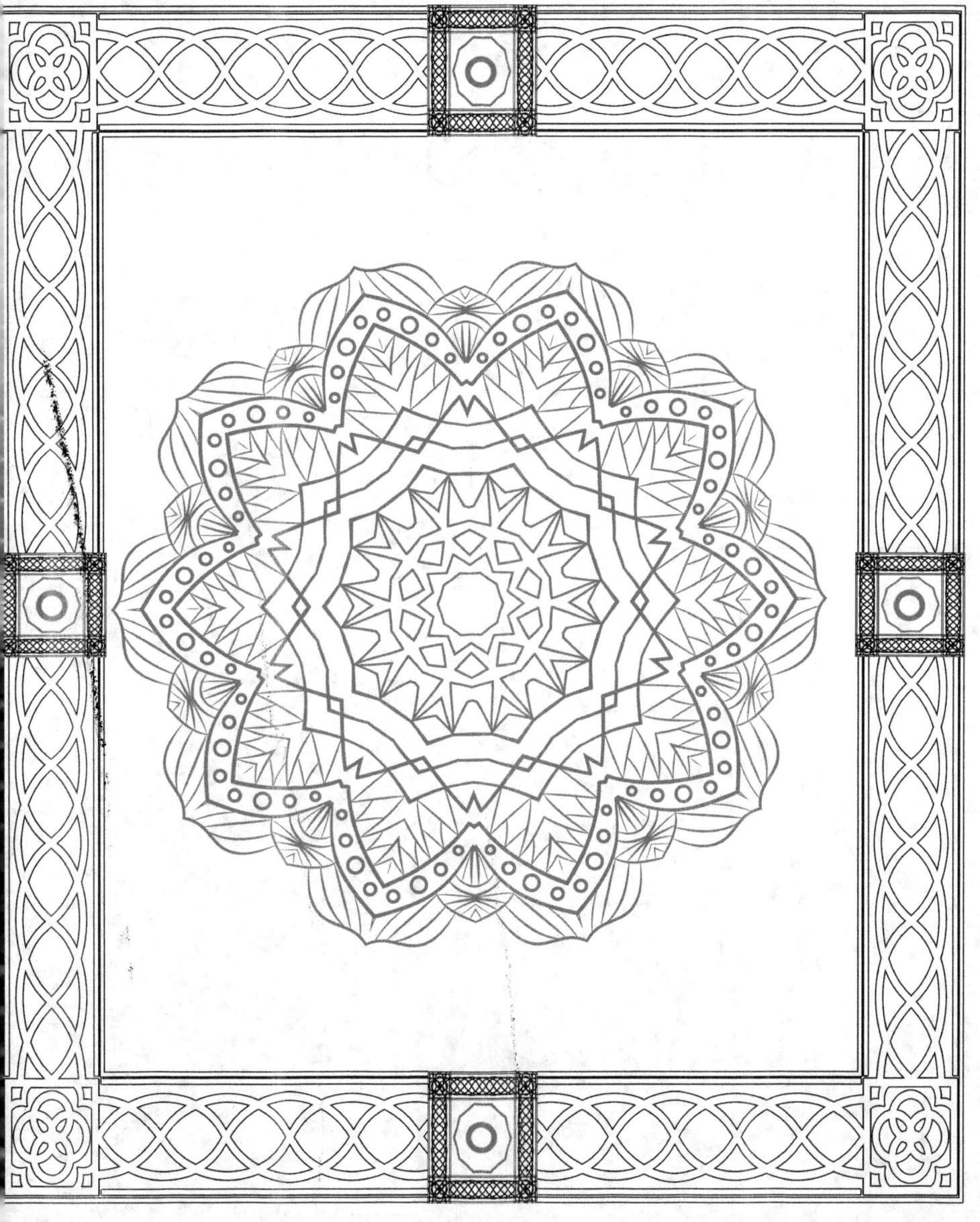

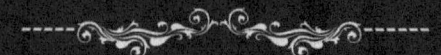

The word 'HAPPINESS' would lose its MEANING

if it were not balanced by SADNESS...

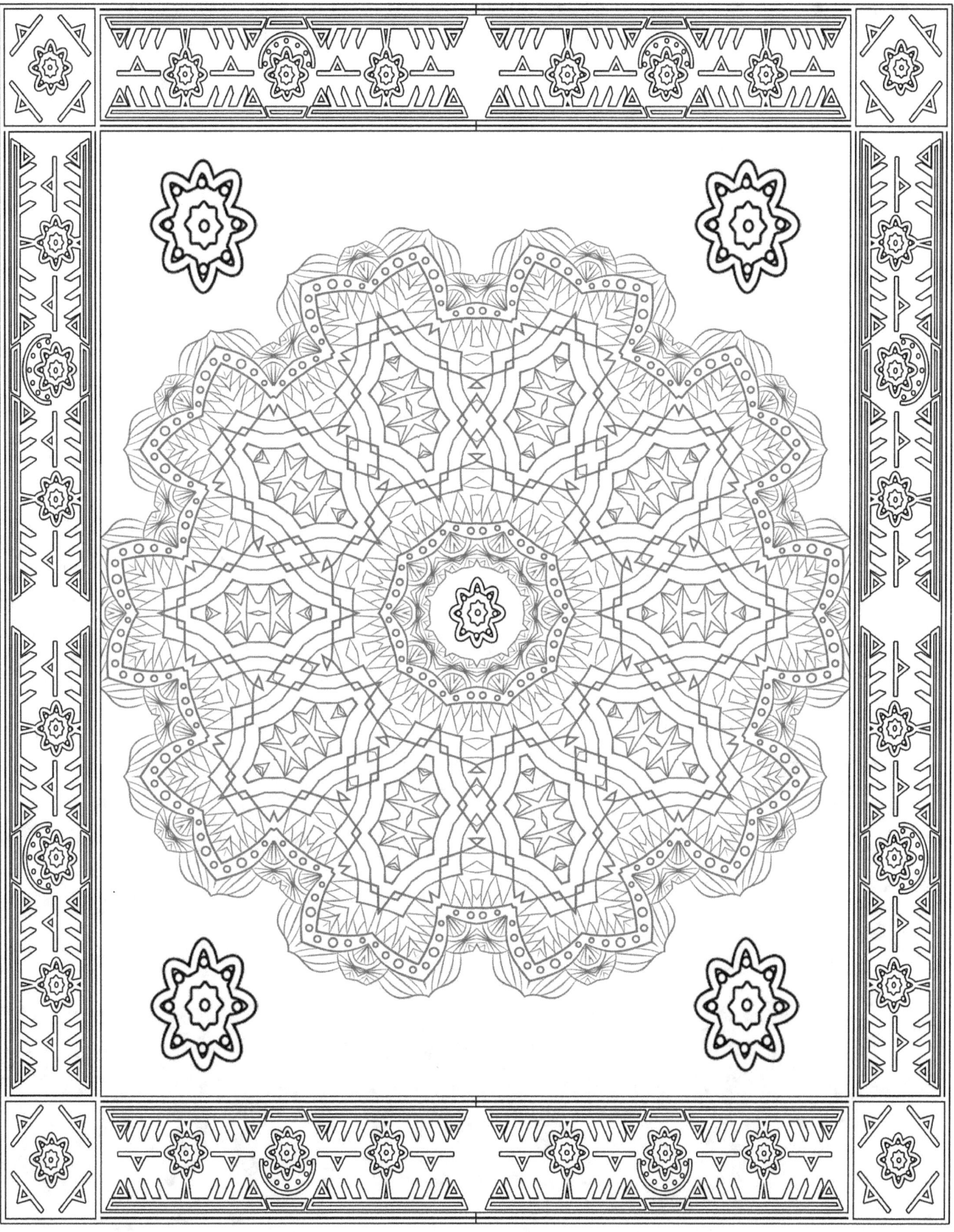

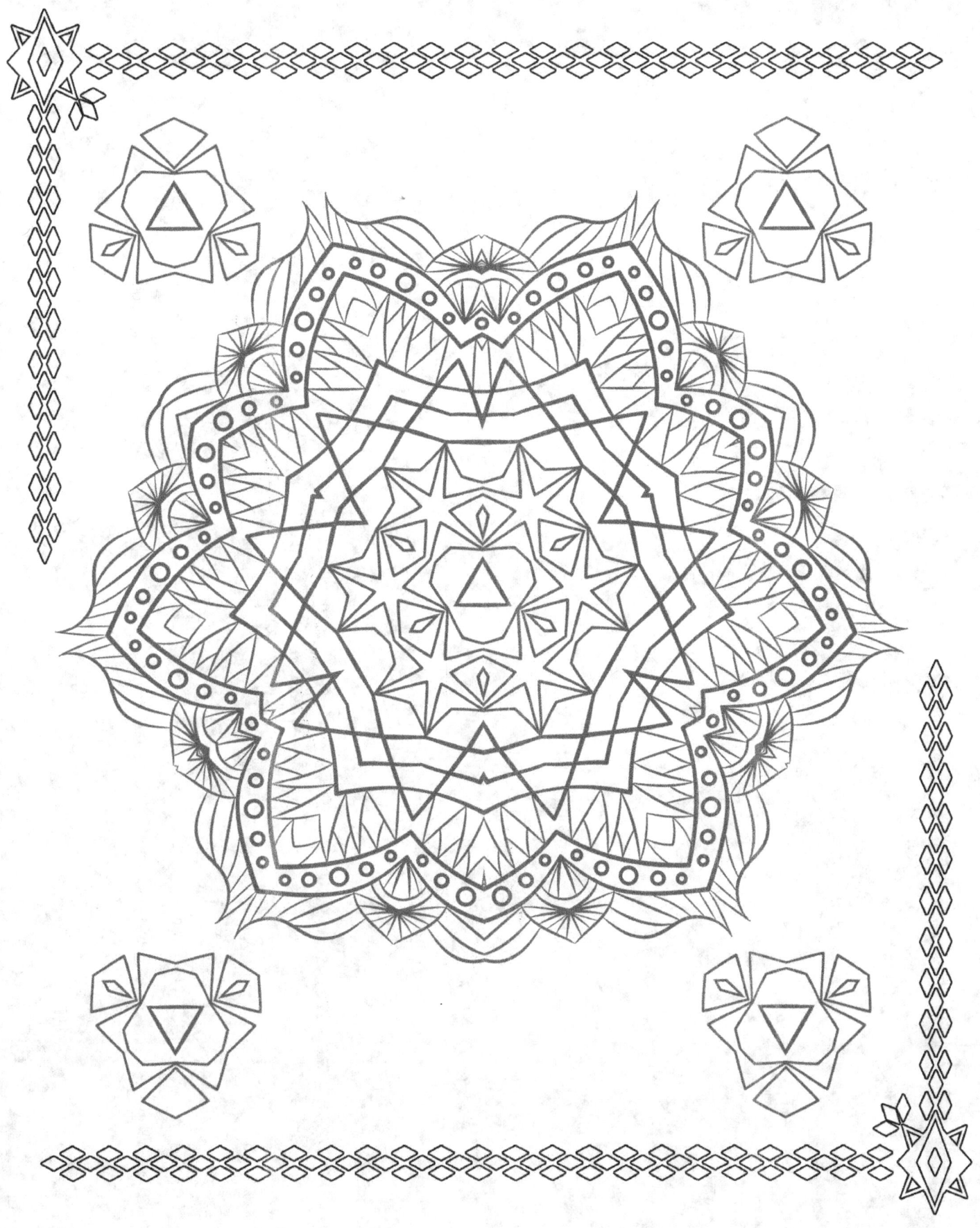

Knowledge rests not upon Truth alone,
but upon Error also.

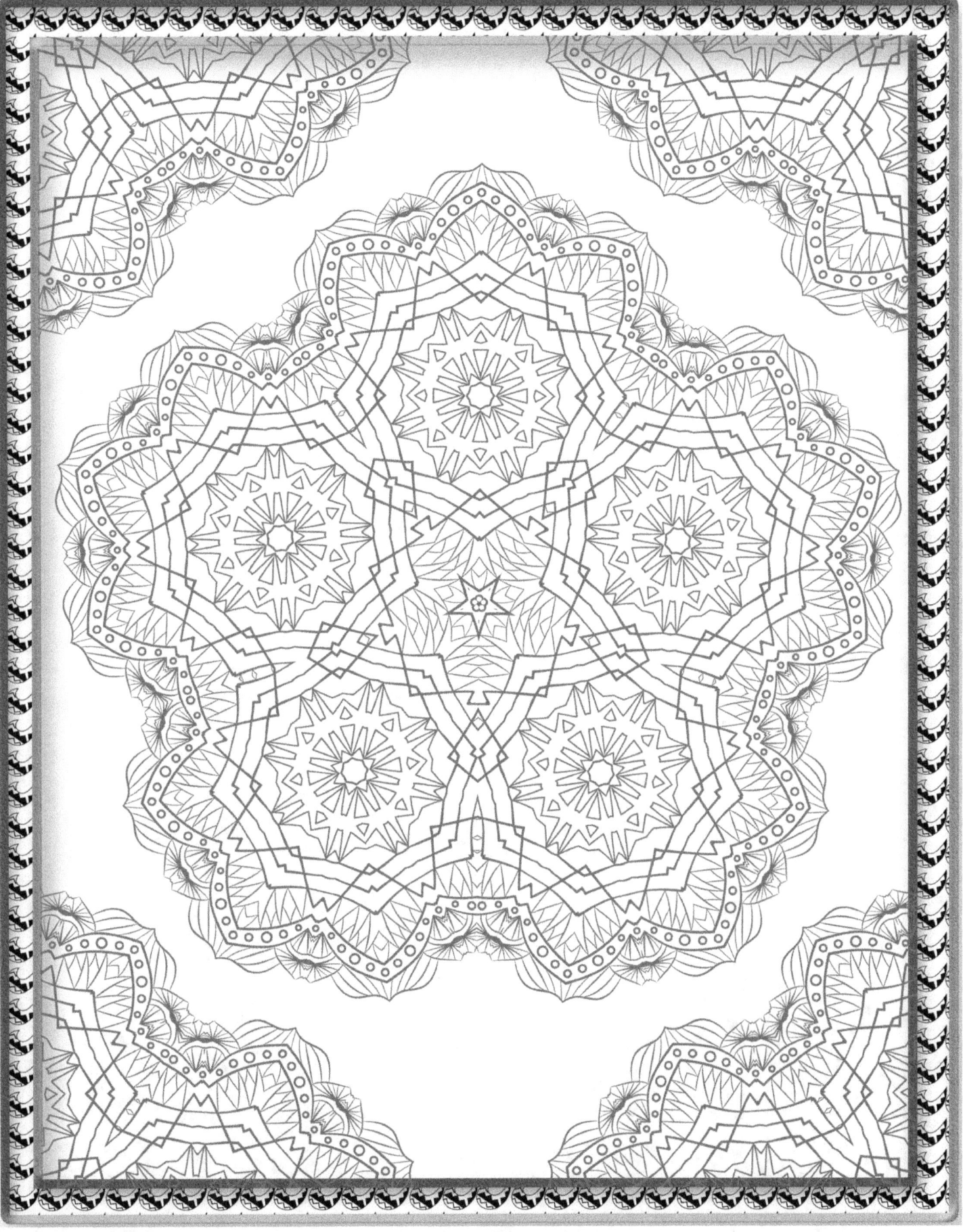

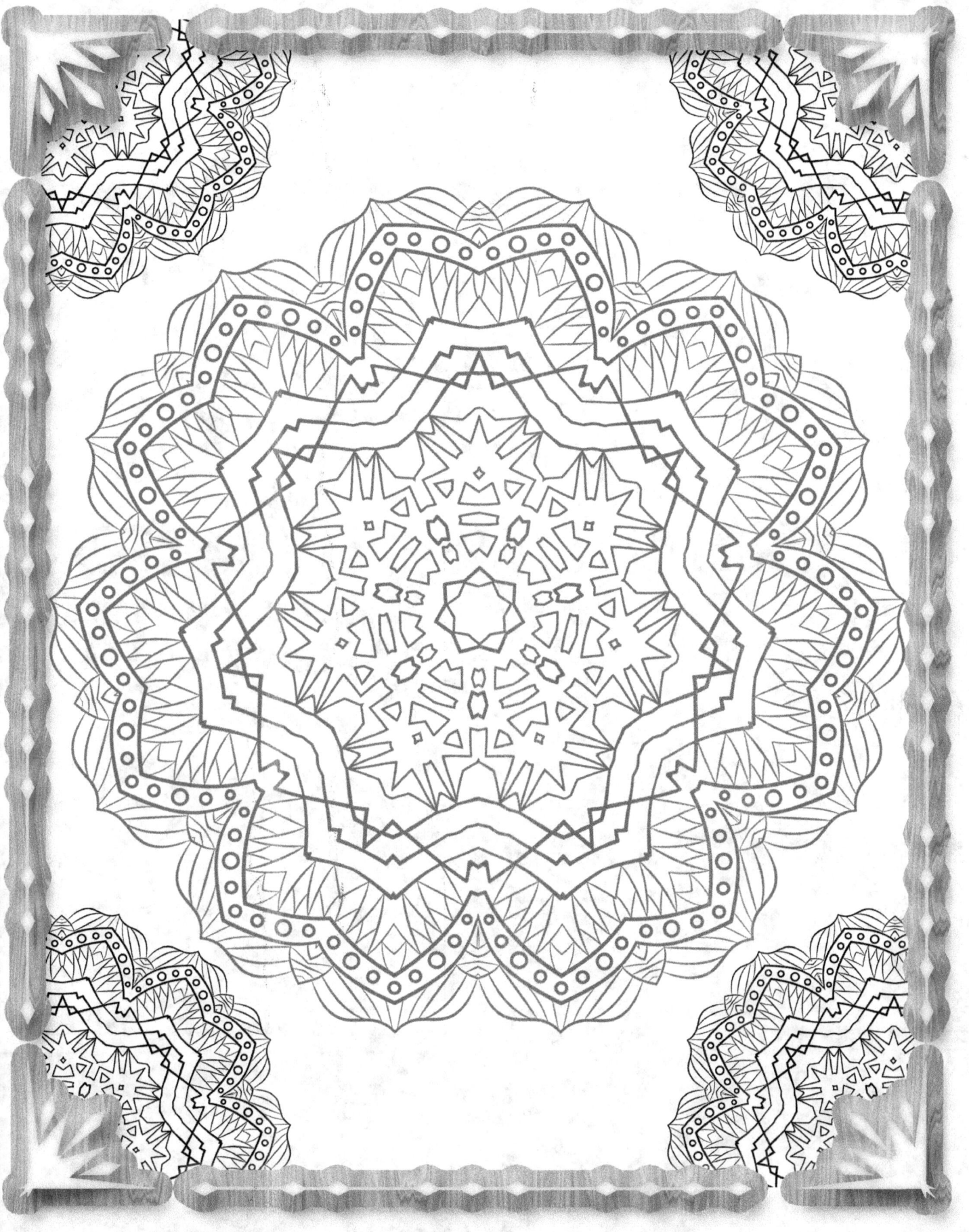

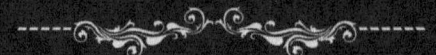

As far as we can discern, the sole
purpose of human existence is to
kindle a light in the darkness of mere being...

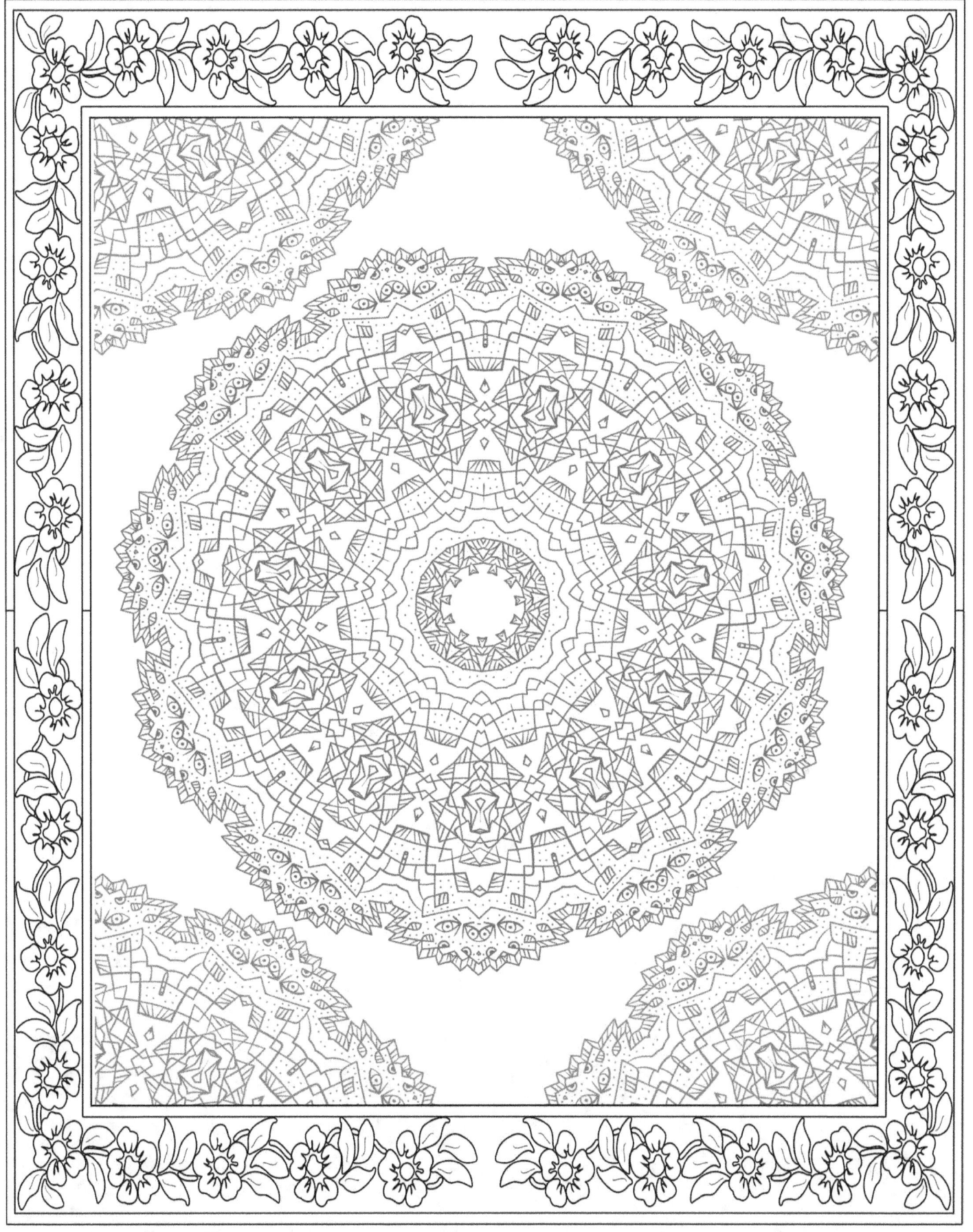

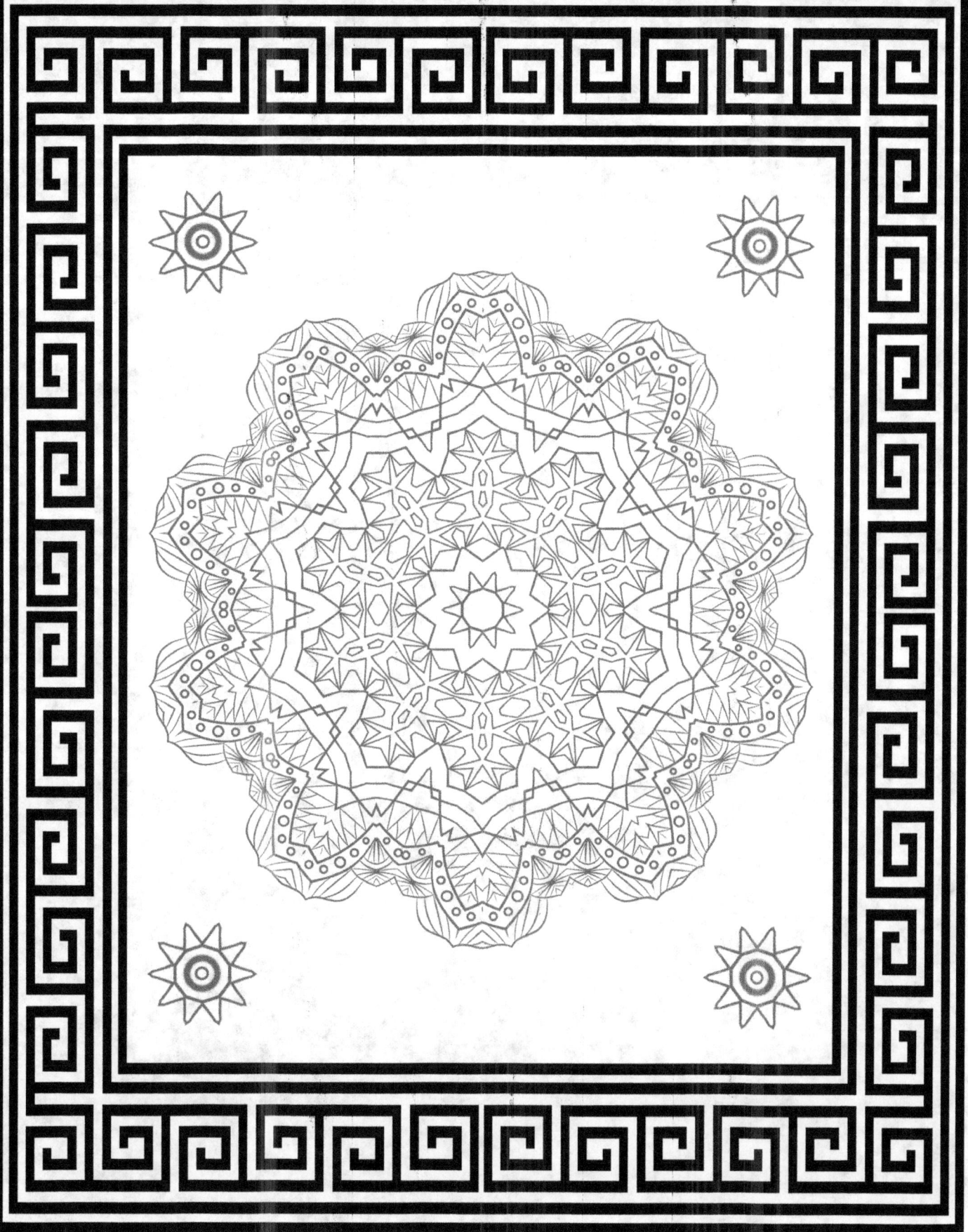

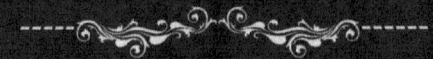

EVERYTHING THAT IRRITATES US ABOUT OTHERS
CAN LEAD US TO AN UNDERSTANDING OF OURSELVES...

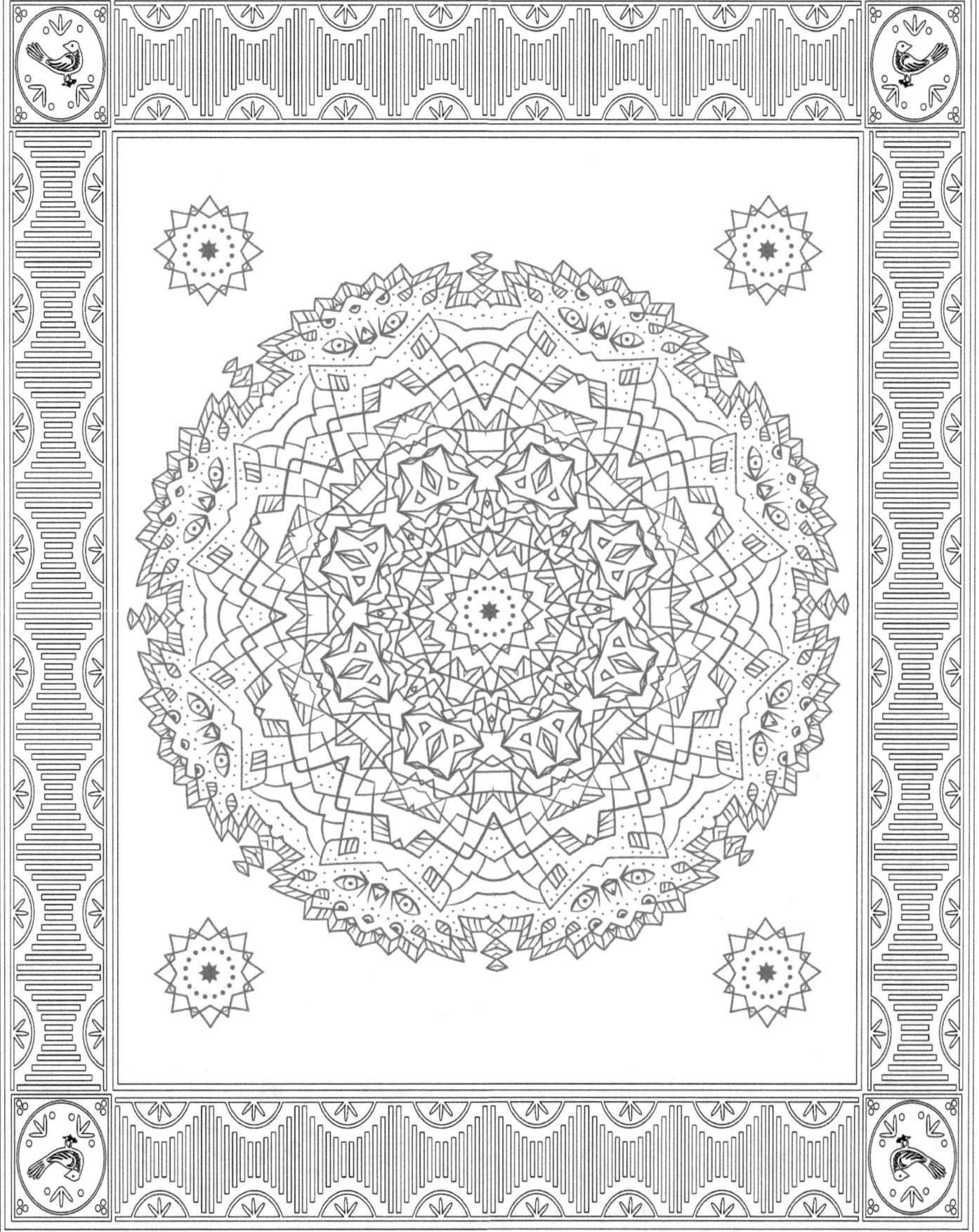

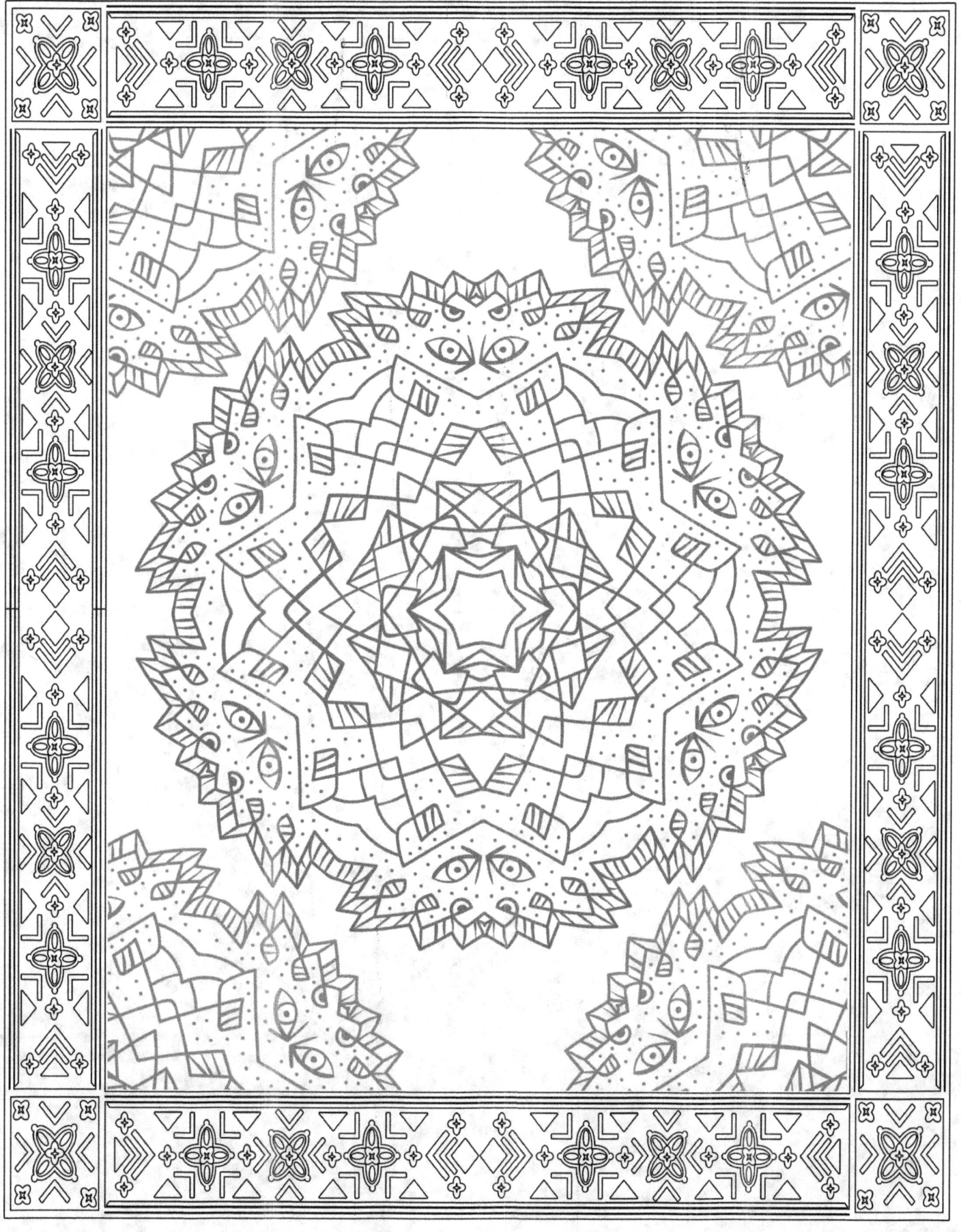

I am not what happened to me,
I am what I choose to become...

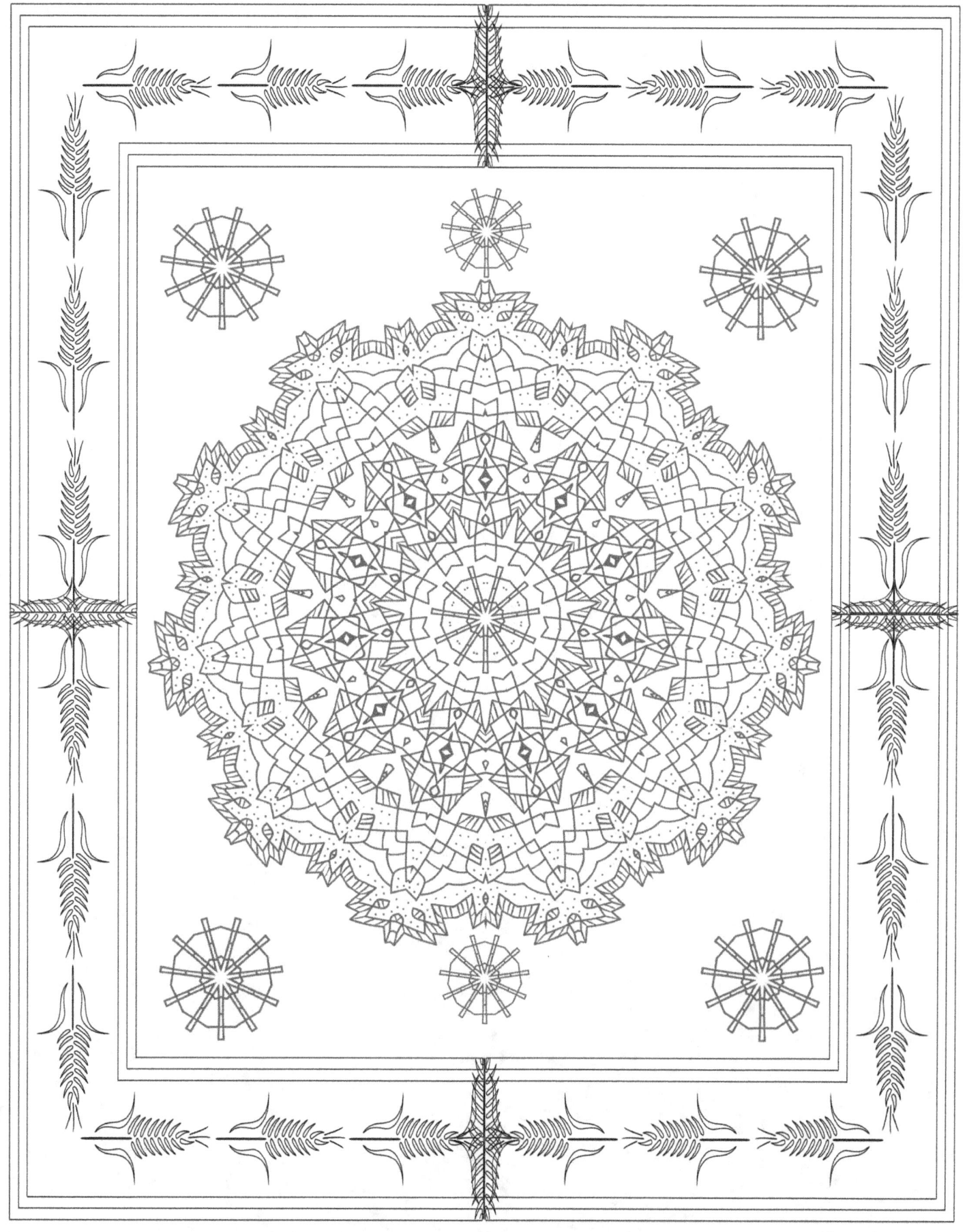

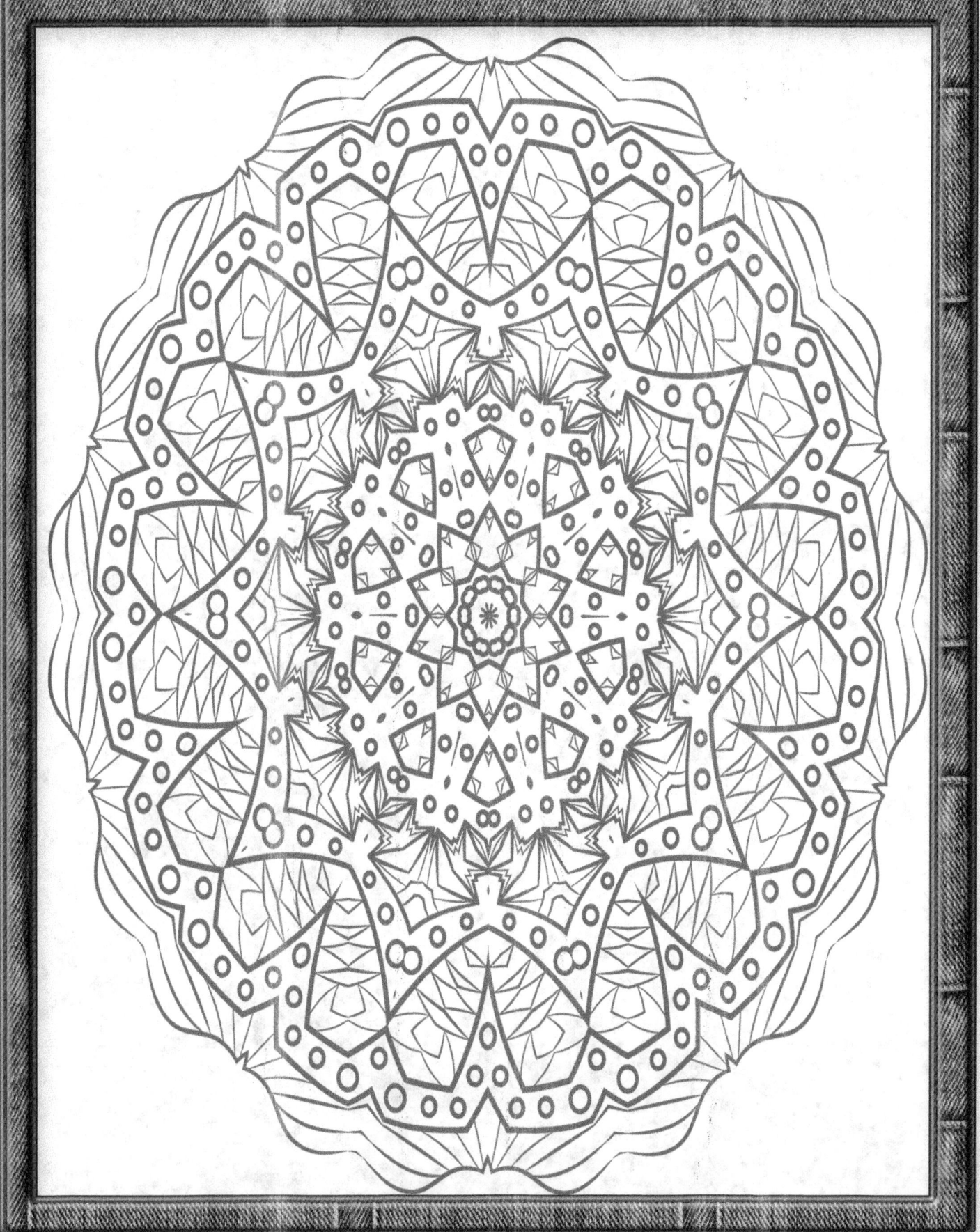

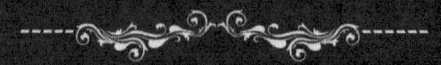

You are what you do,
not what you say you'll do...

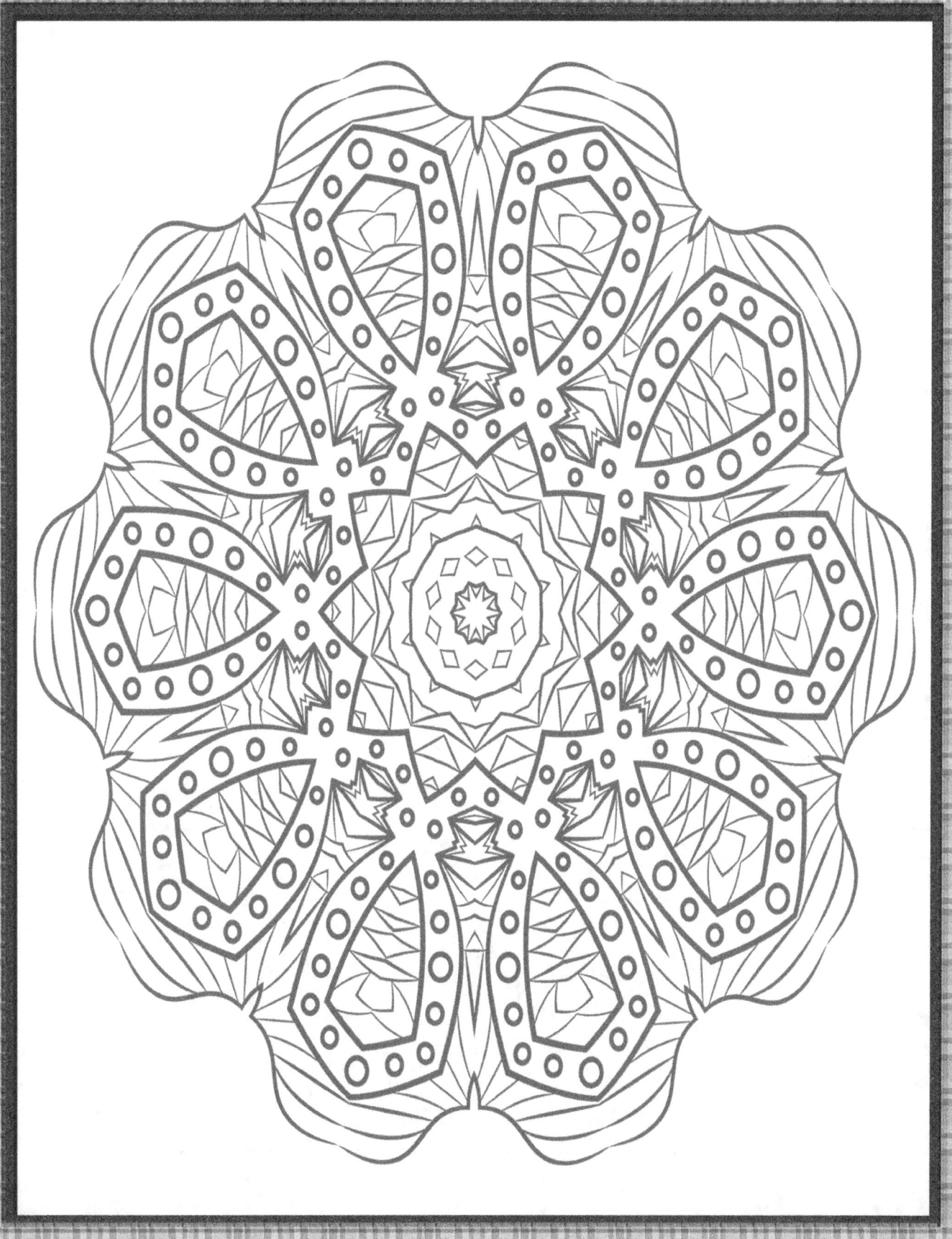

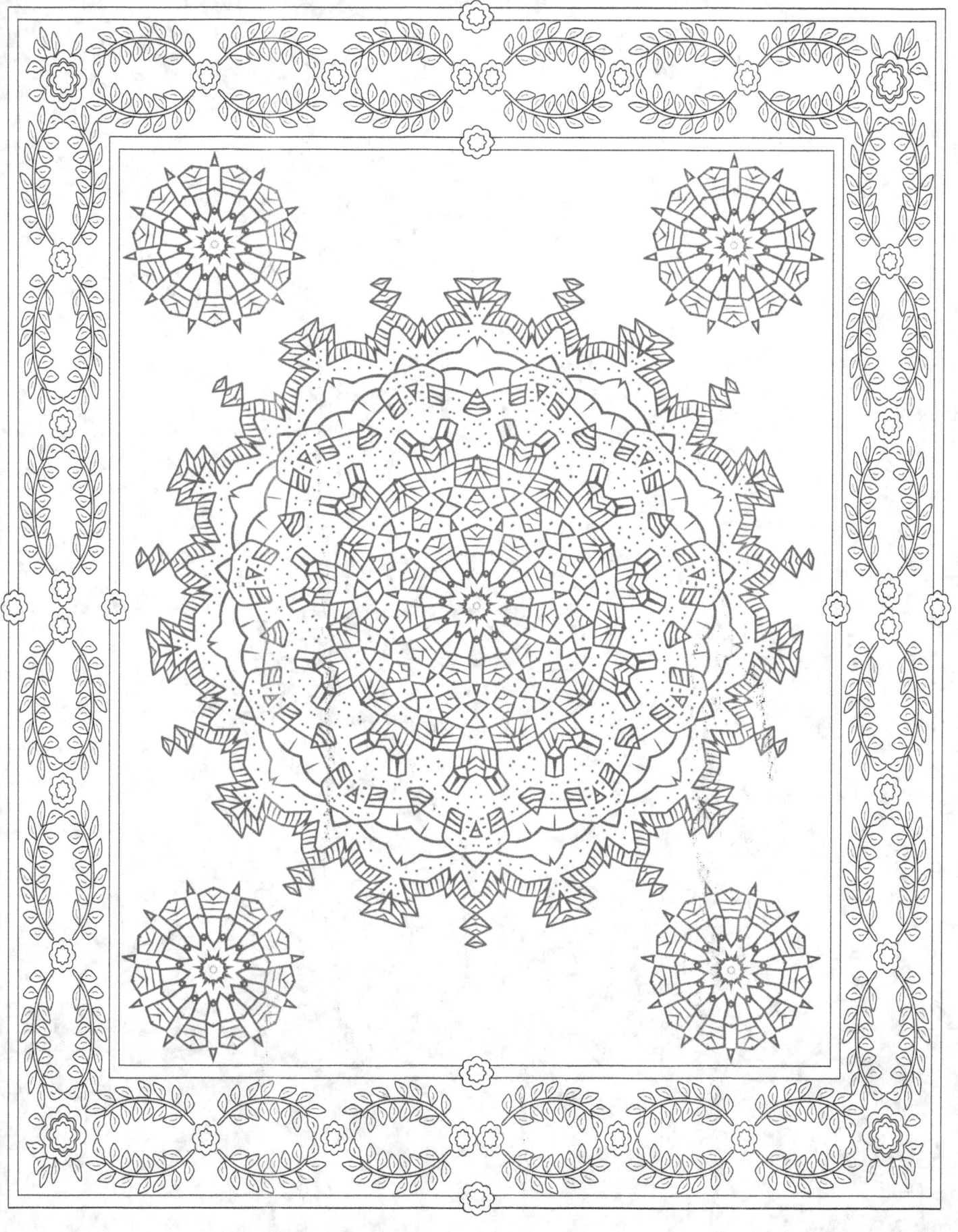

Knowing your own darkness
is the best method for dealing with the
darknesses of other people

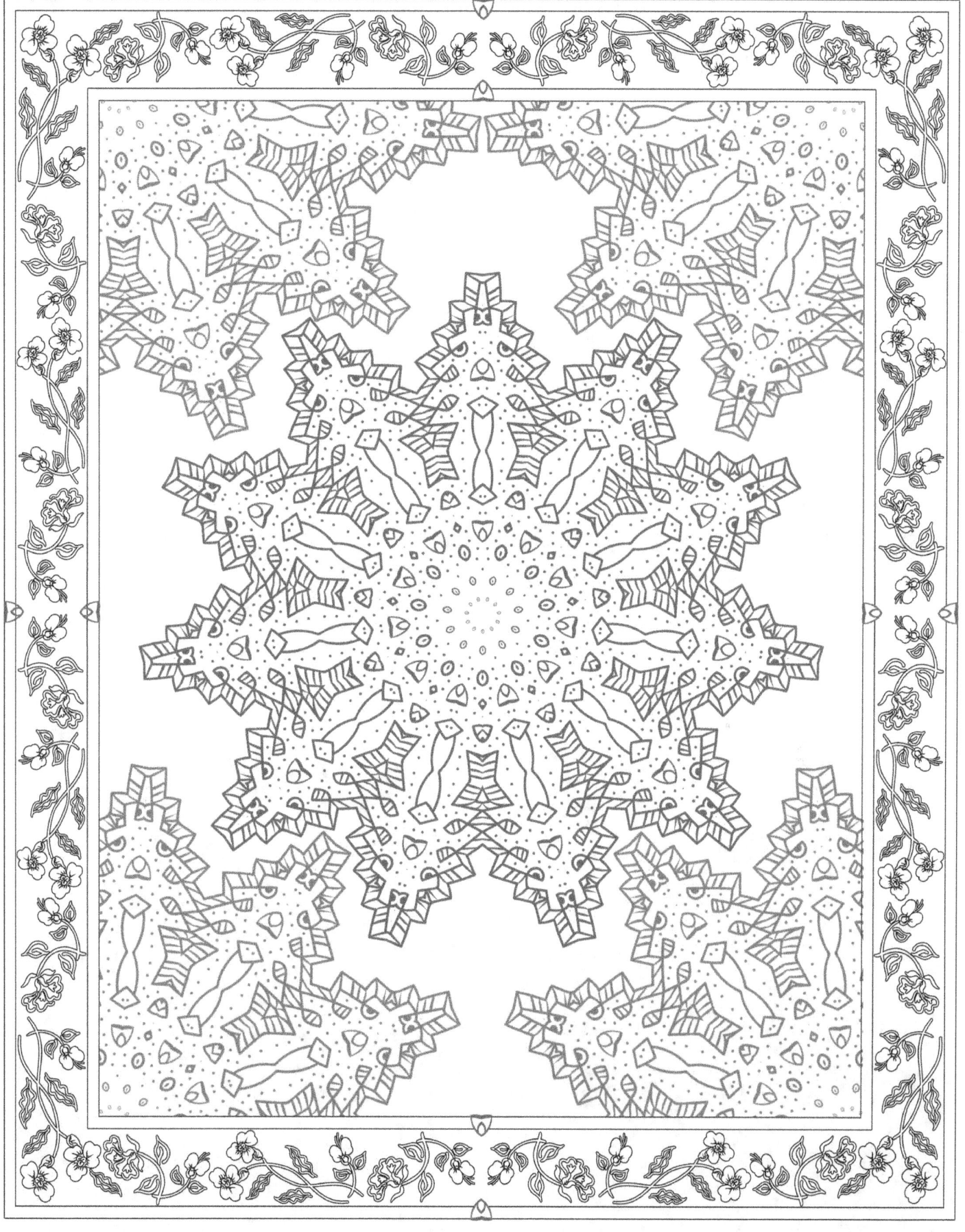

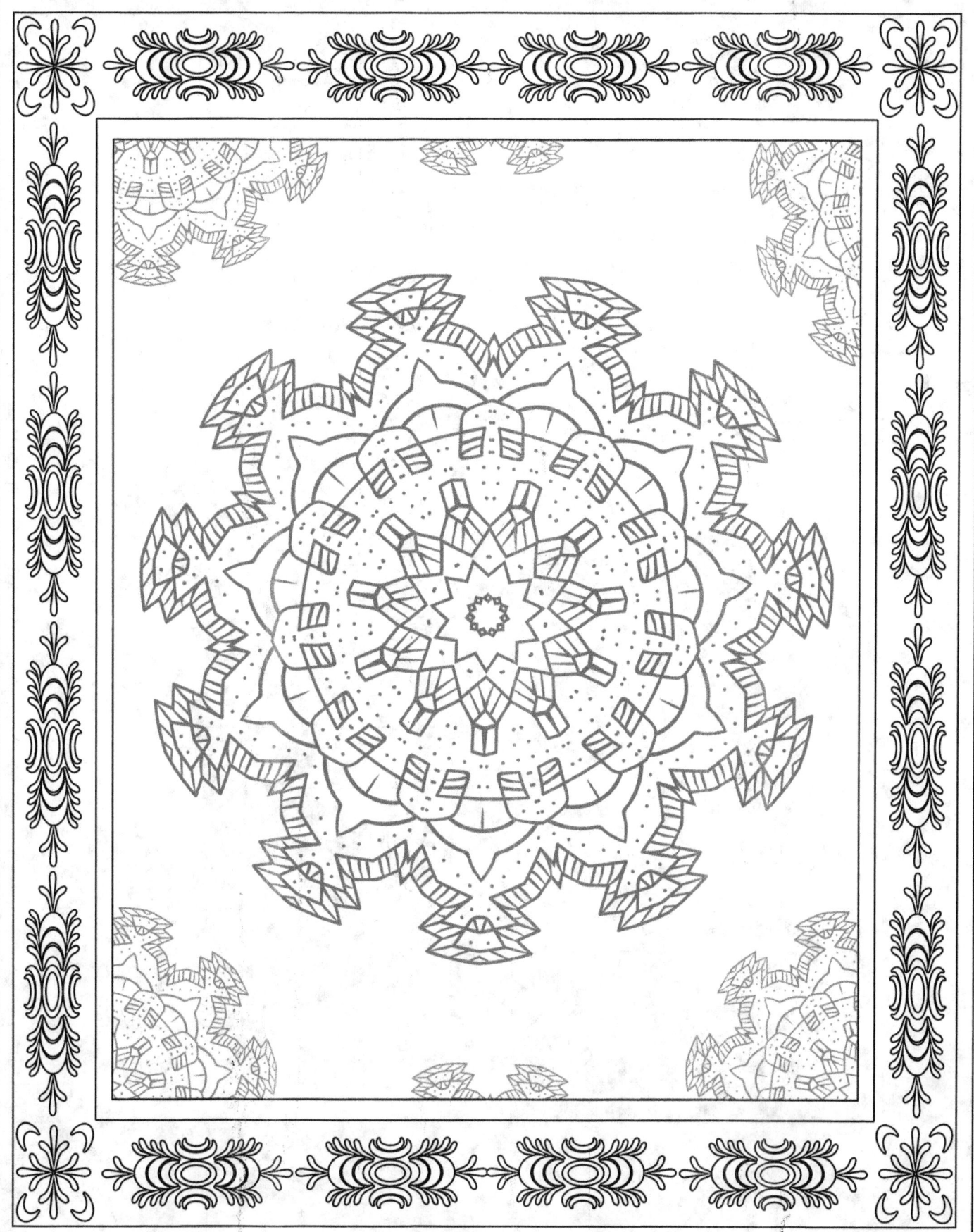

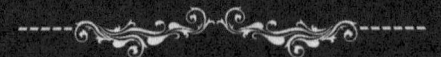

THE PENDULUM OF THE MIND OSCILLATES
BETWEEN SENSE AND NONSENSE
NOT BETWEEN RIGHT AND WRONG...

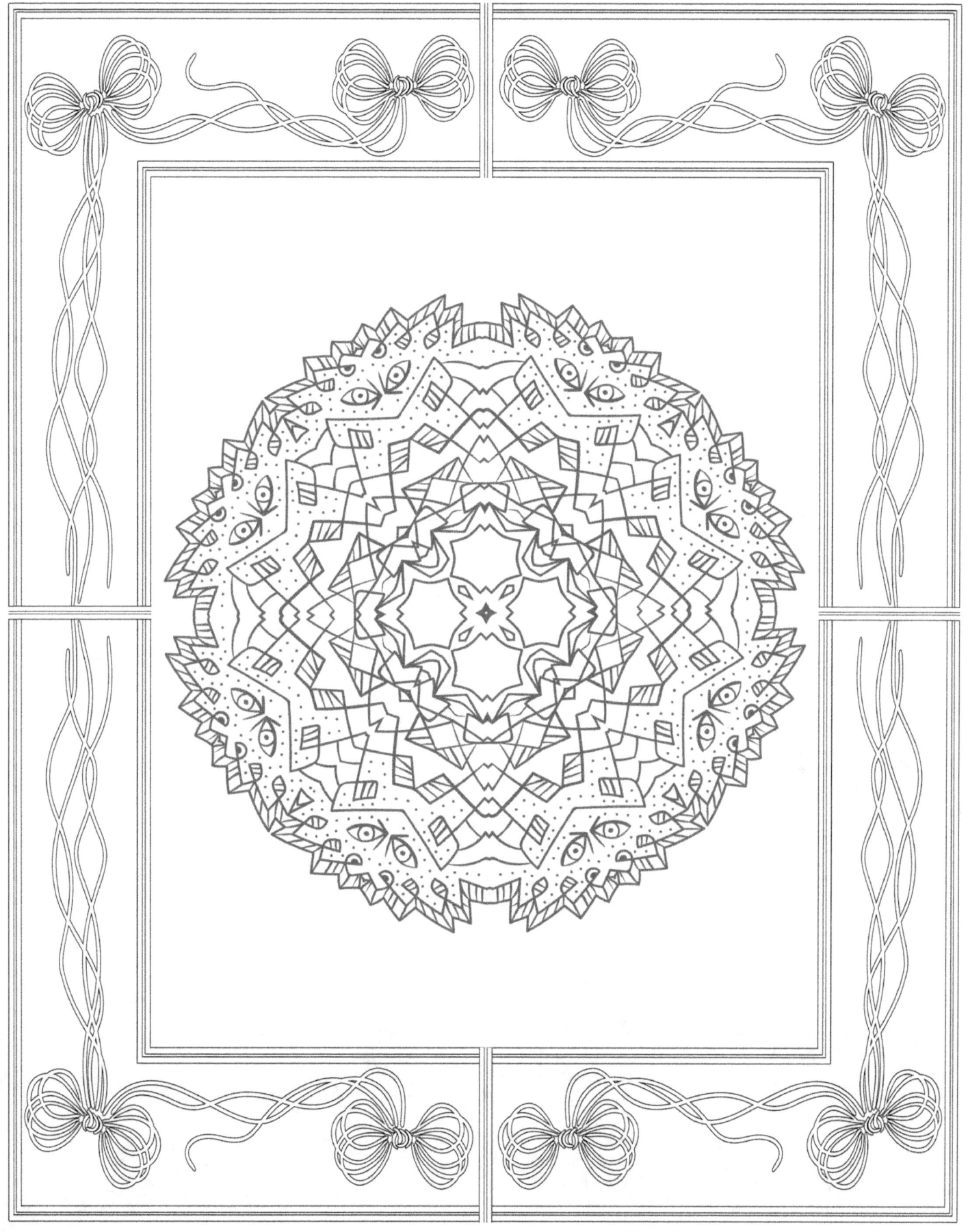

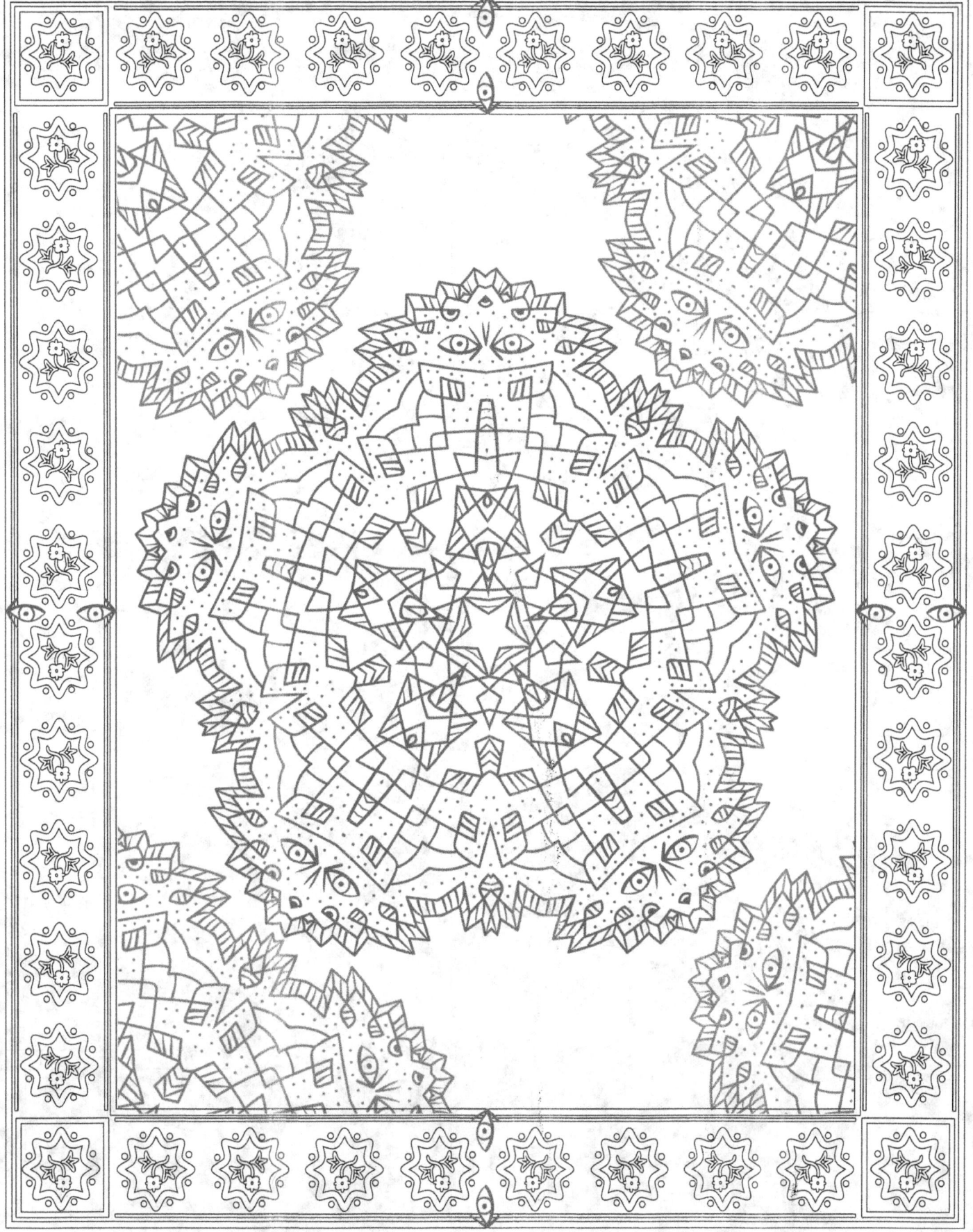

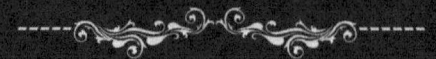

Until you make the unconscious conscious,
it will direct your life and you will call it fate

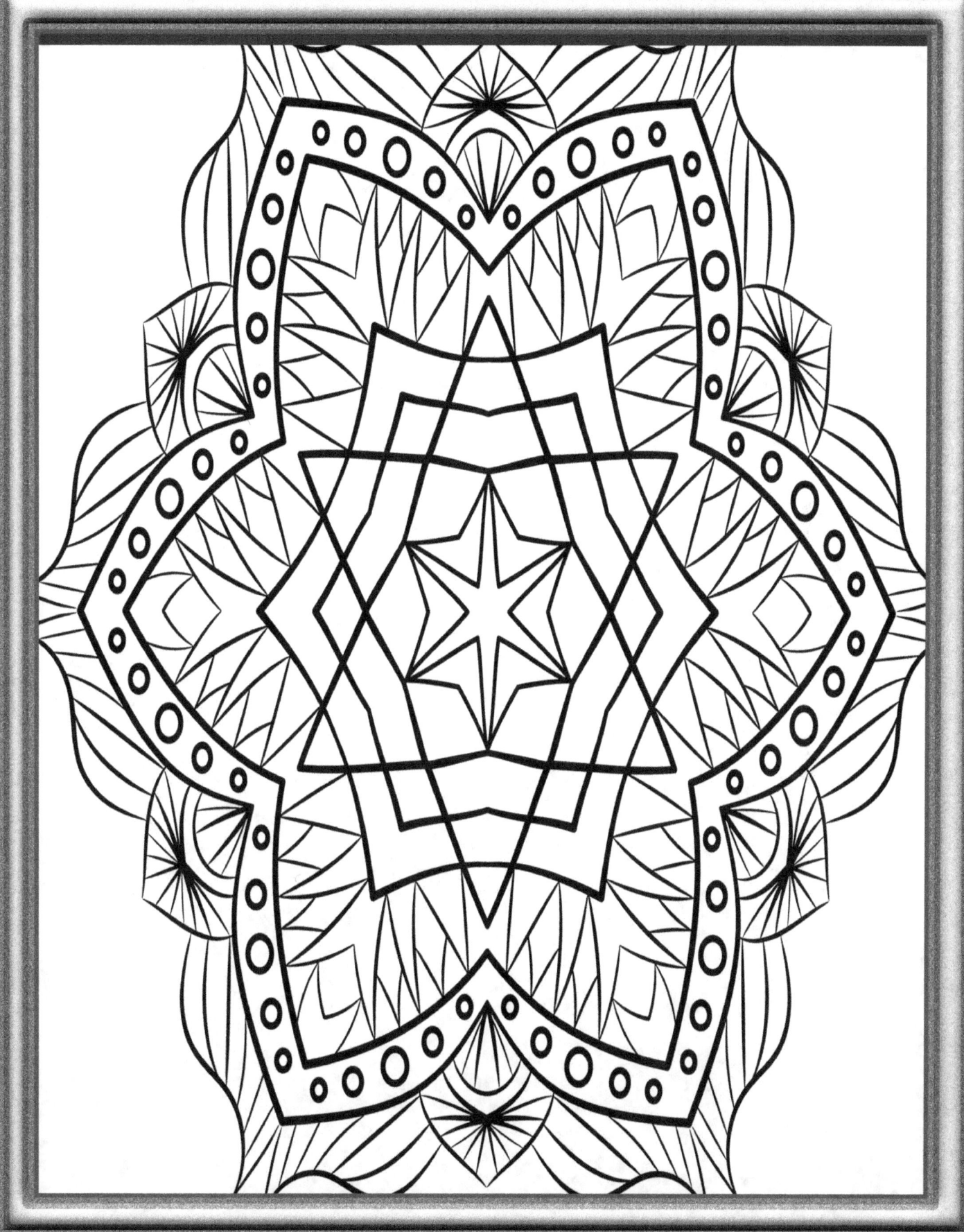

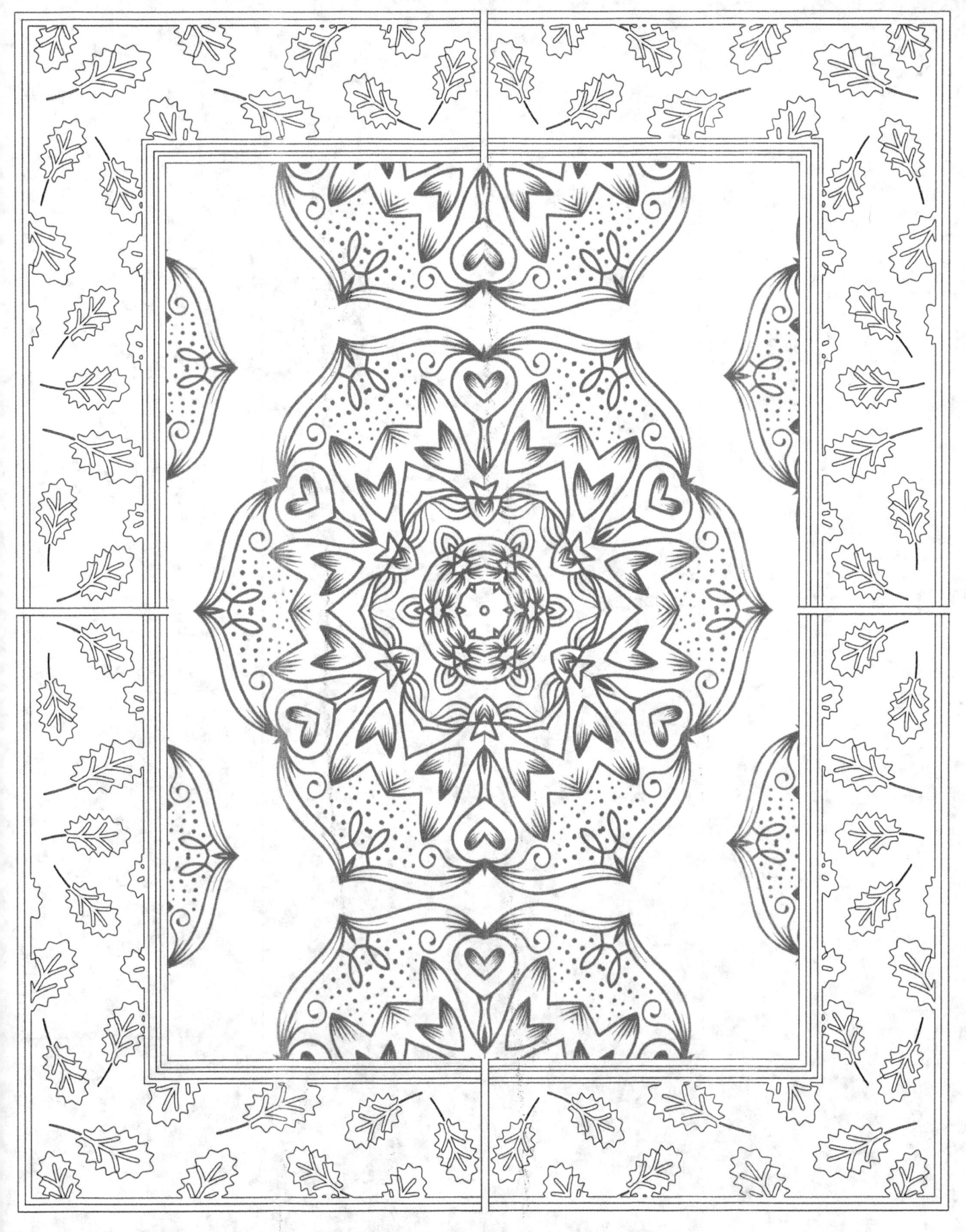

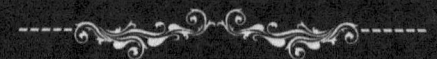

THE privilege OF A lifETiME iS TO bEcOME whO yOu Truly ArE.

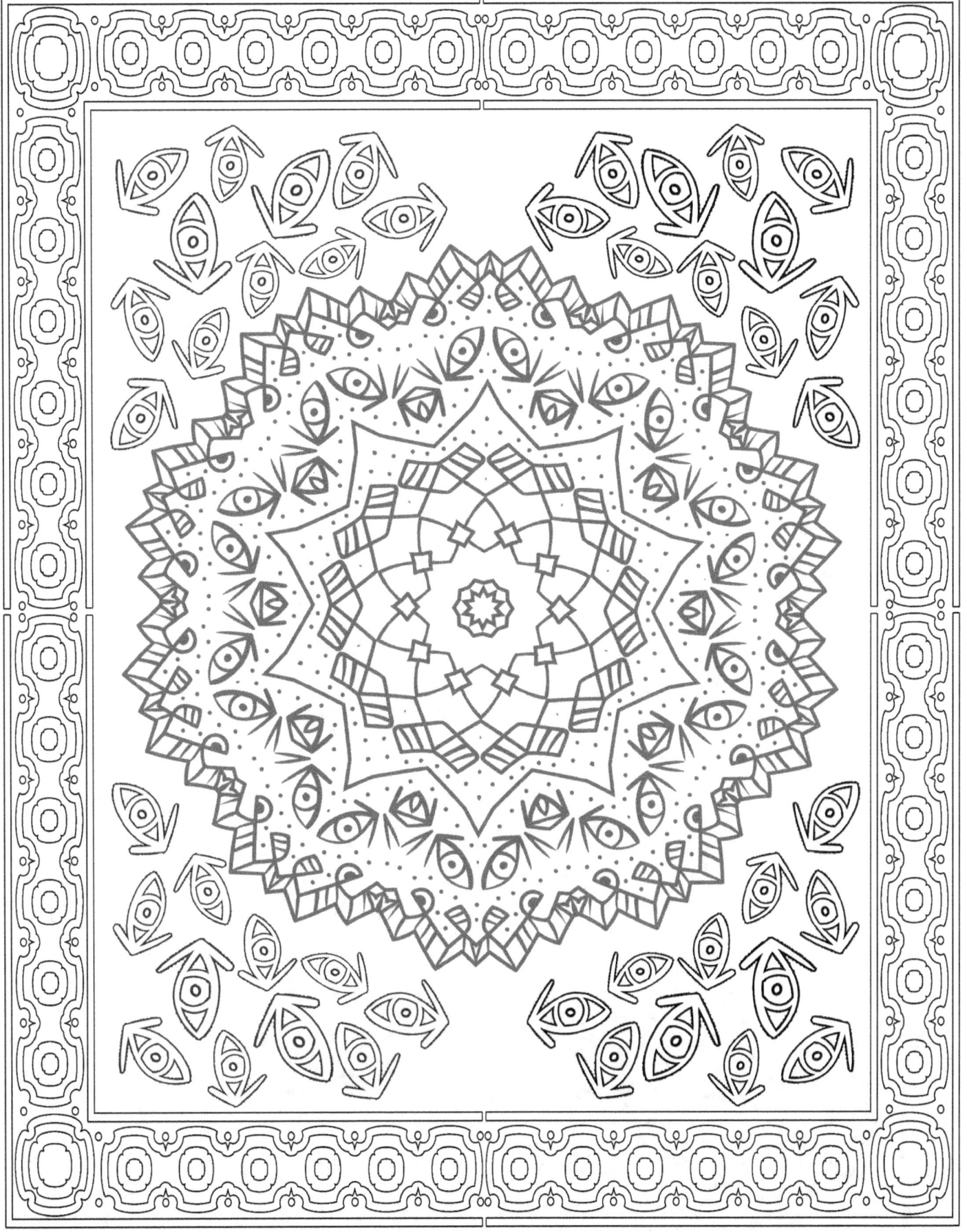

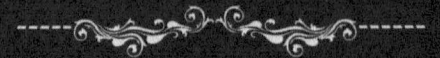

PEoplE will do ANyThing, no MATTEr how AbSurd,

To Avoid FACing THEir own SoulS

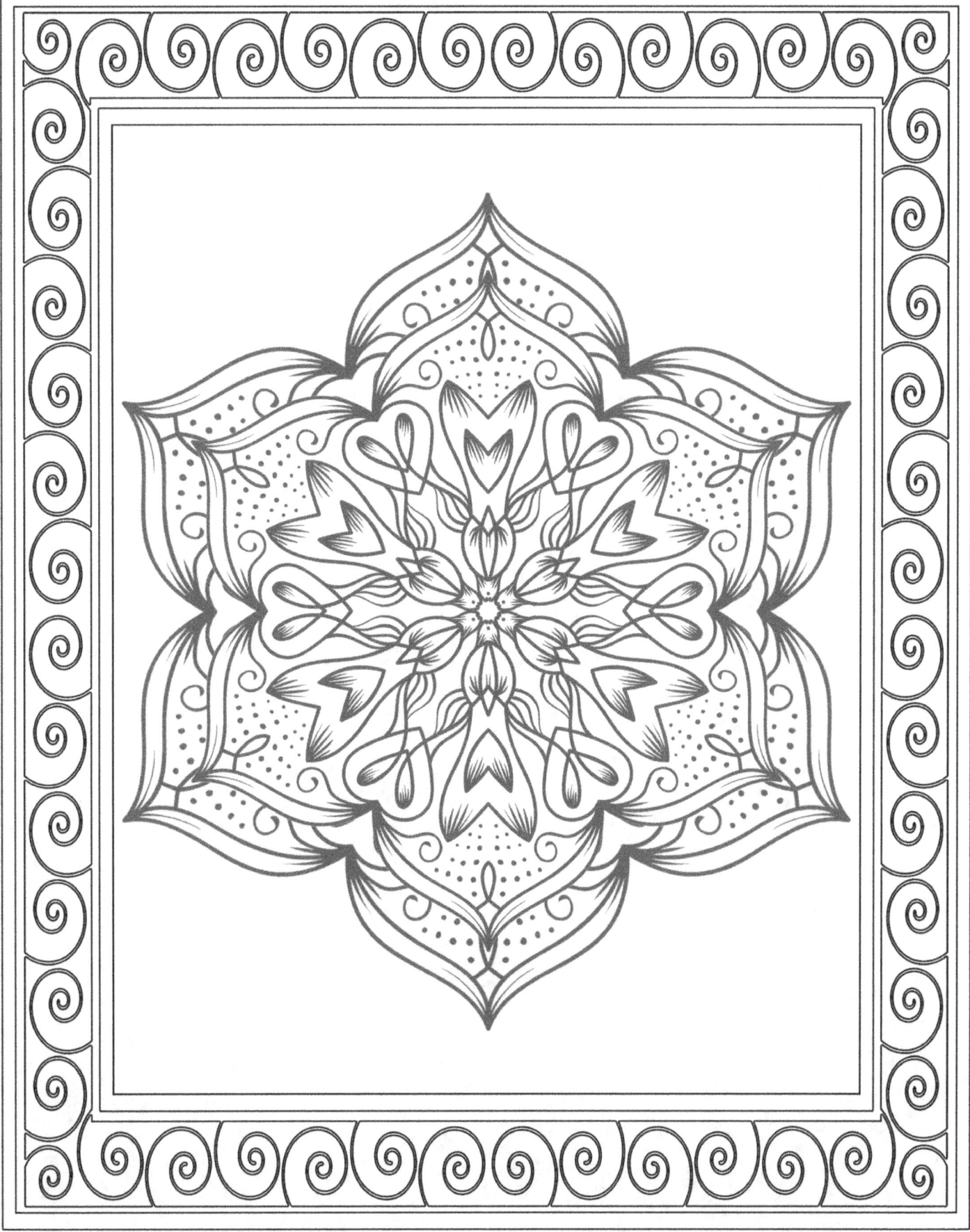

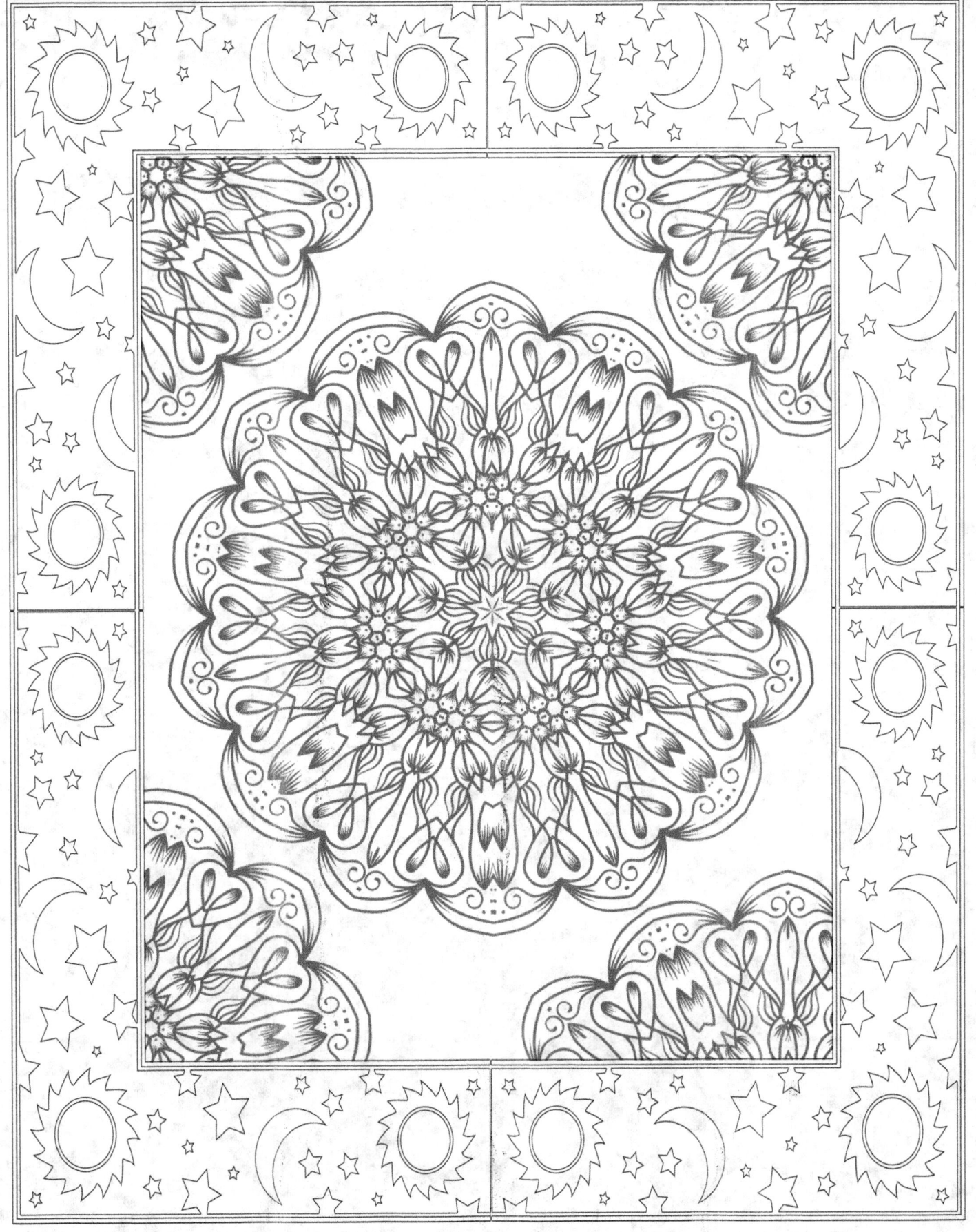

THE MOST TERRIFYING THING IS TO ACCEPT ONESELF COMPLETELY

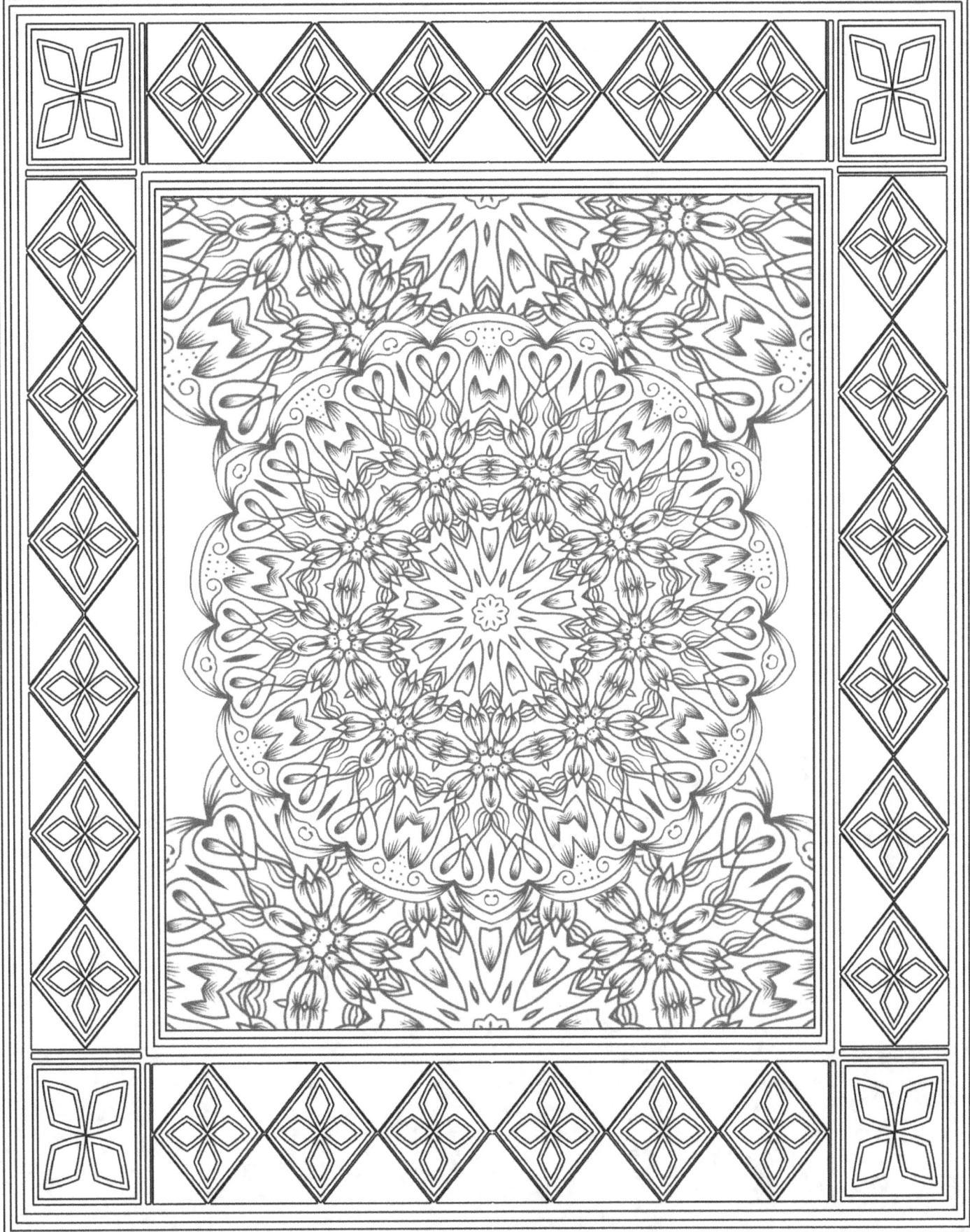

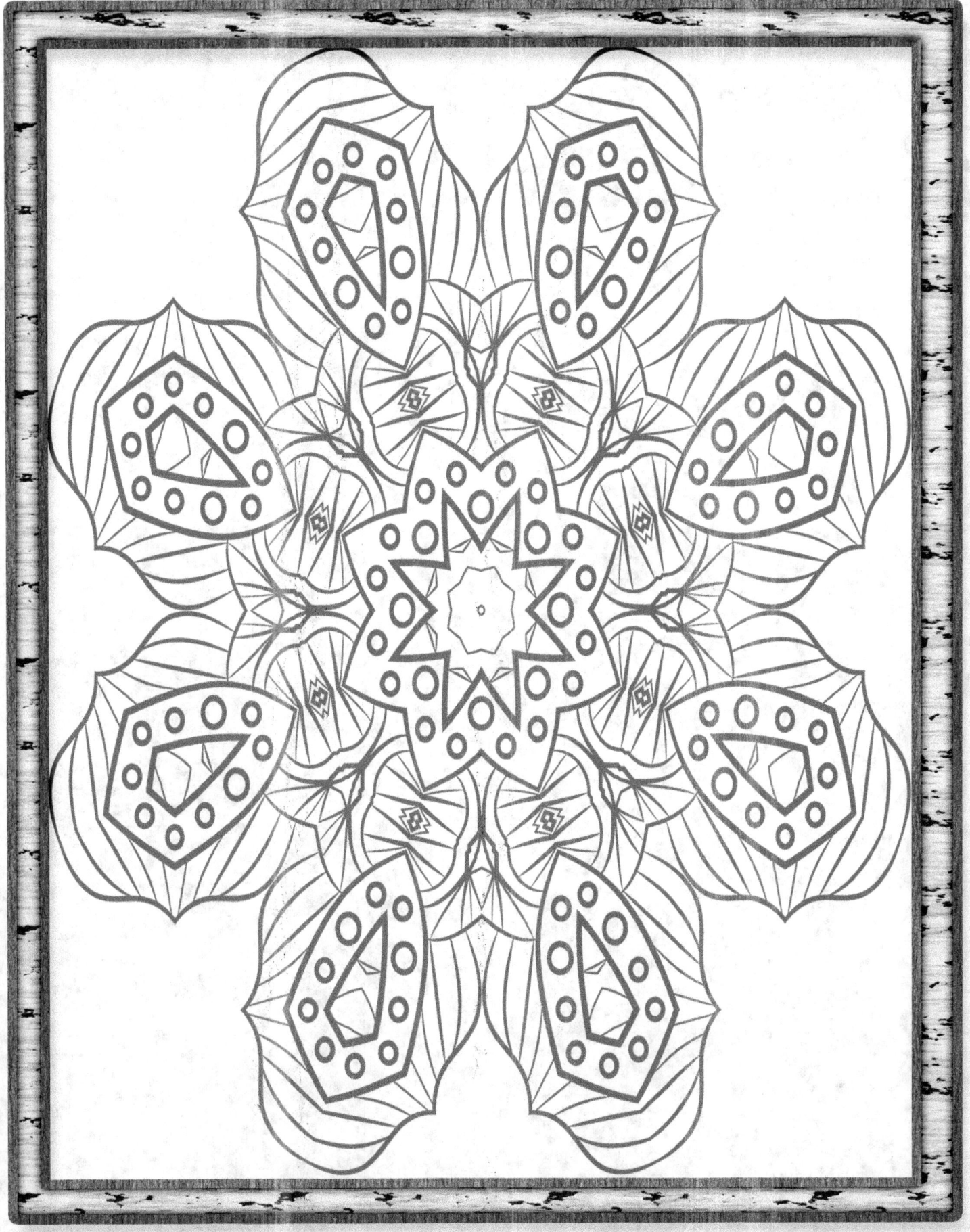

Show me a sane man and I will cure him for you...

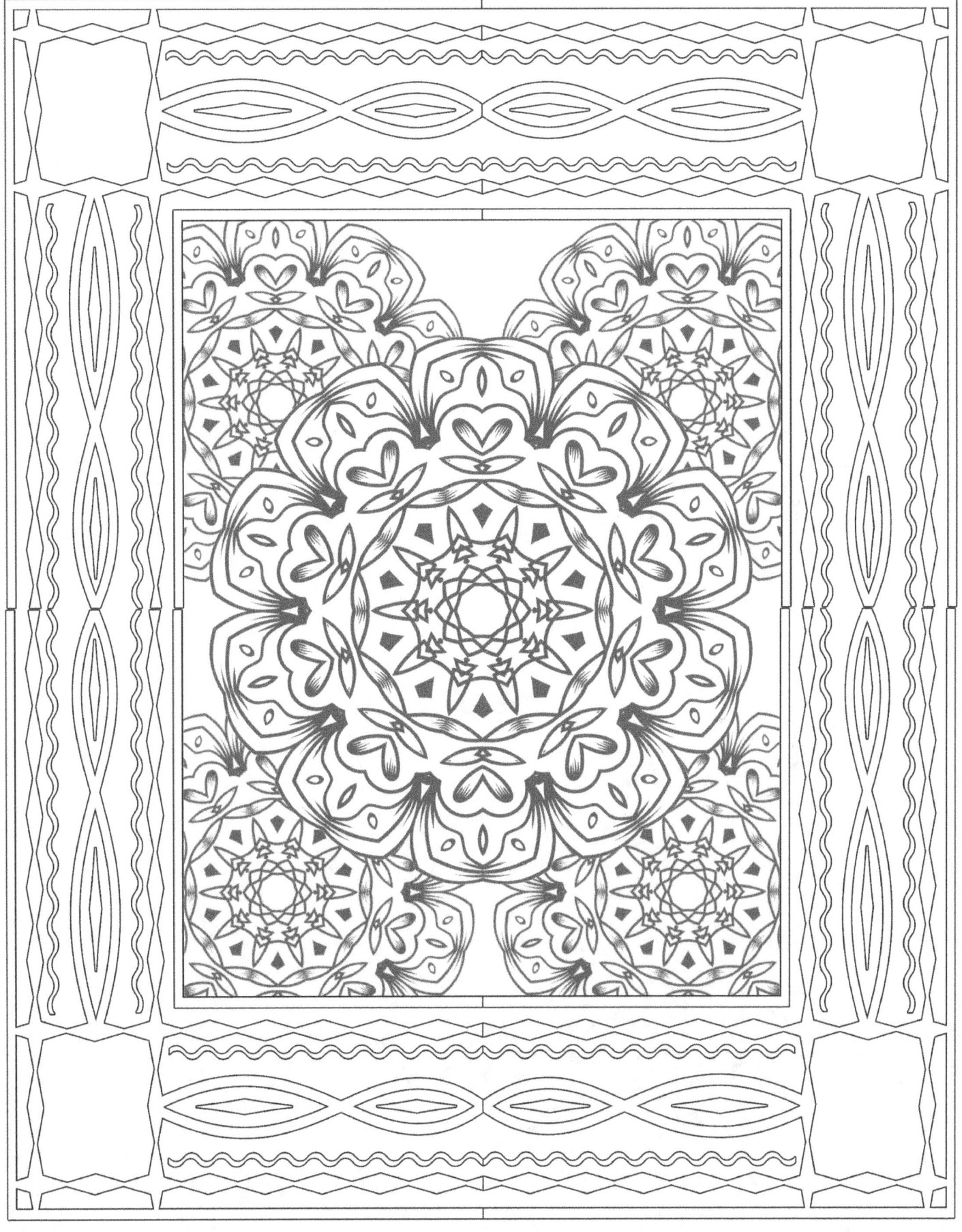

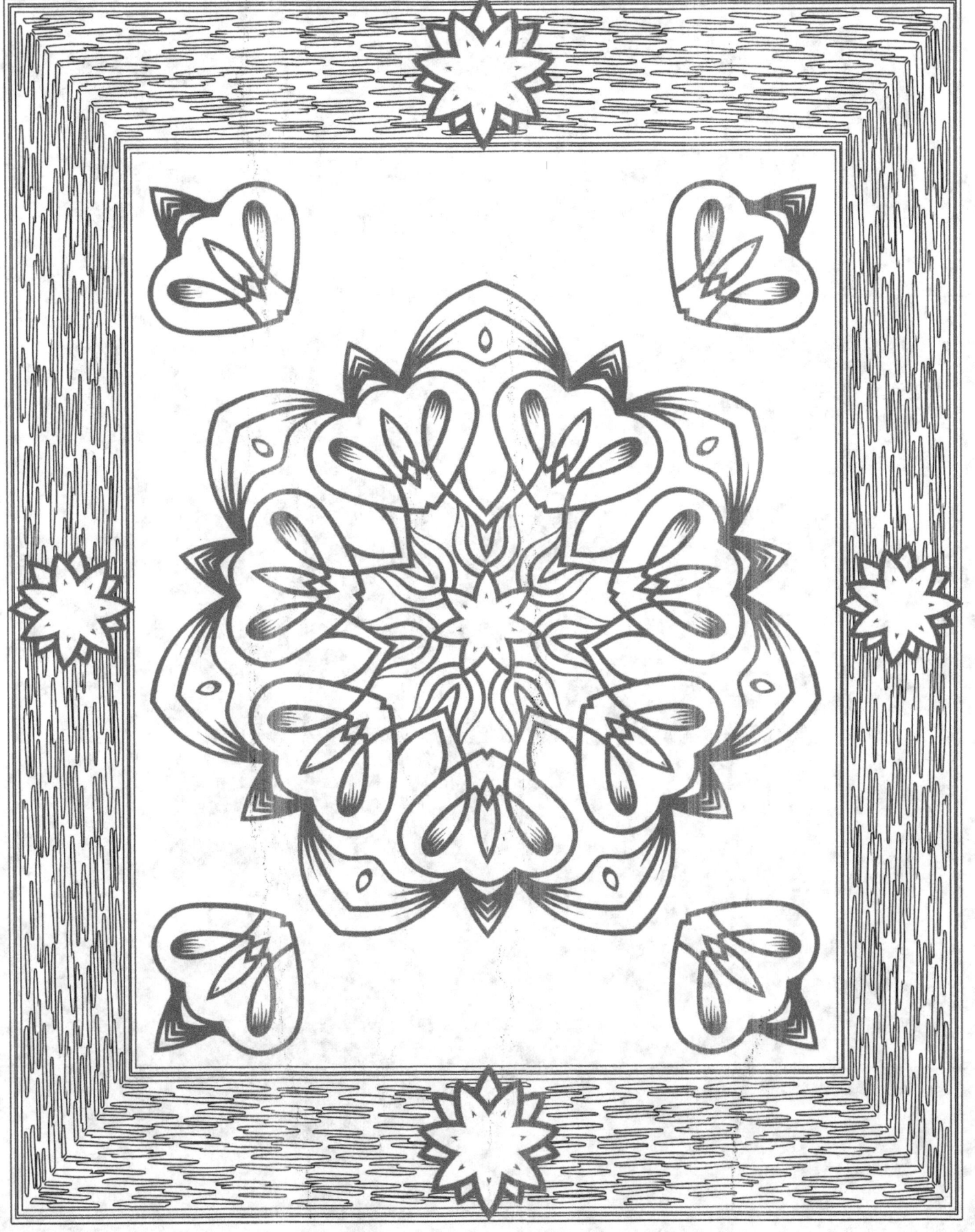

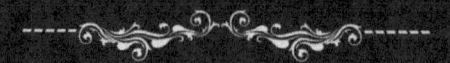

There's no coming to consciousness without pain...

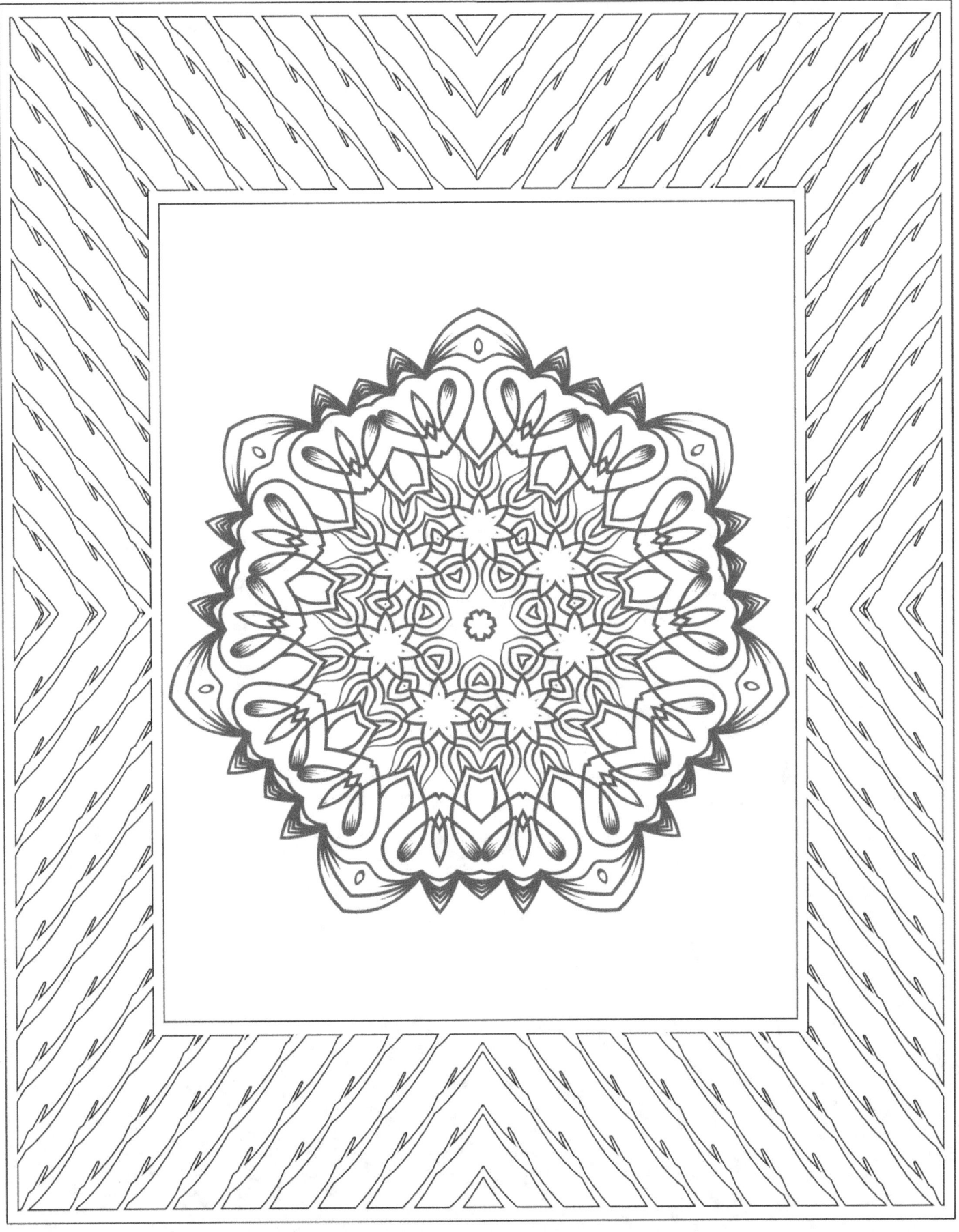

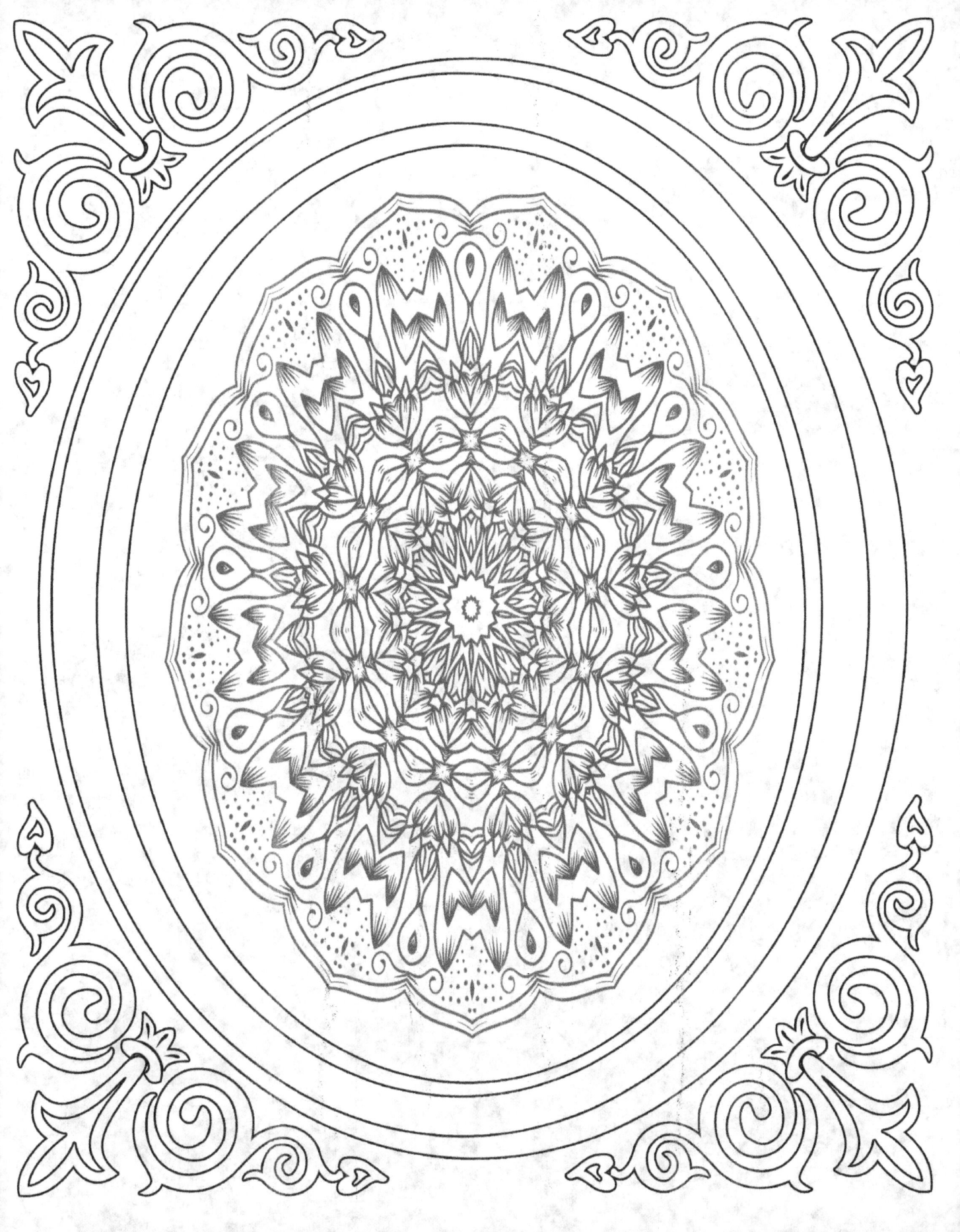

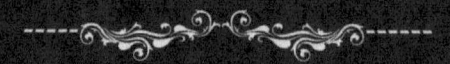

In all chaos there is a cosmos,
in all disorder a secret order

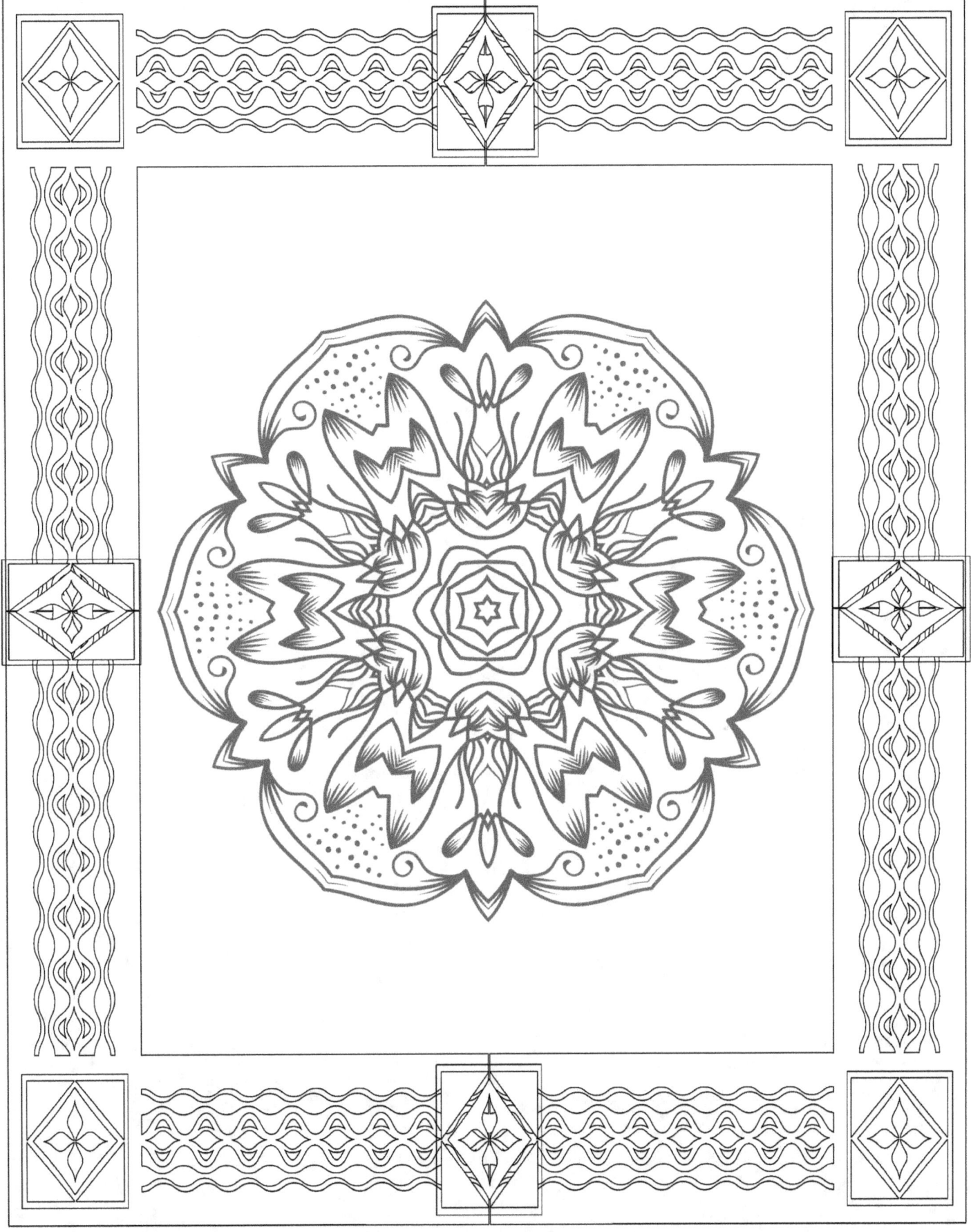

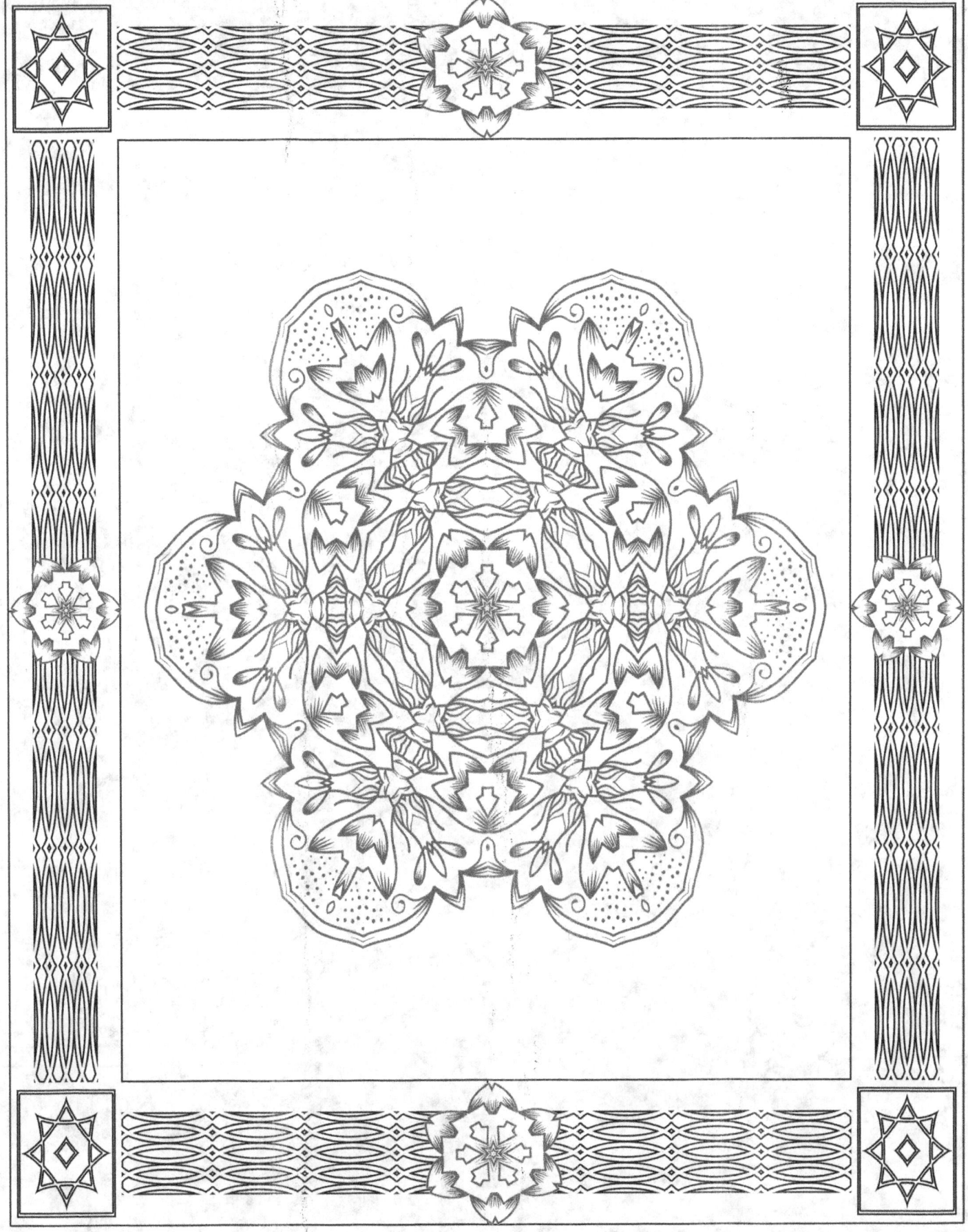

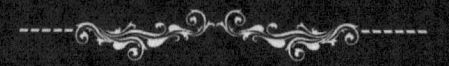

WHATEVEr iS rEJECTEd FrOM THE SEIF,

APPEArS iN THE world AS AN EVENT...

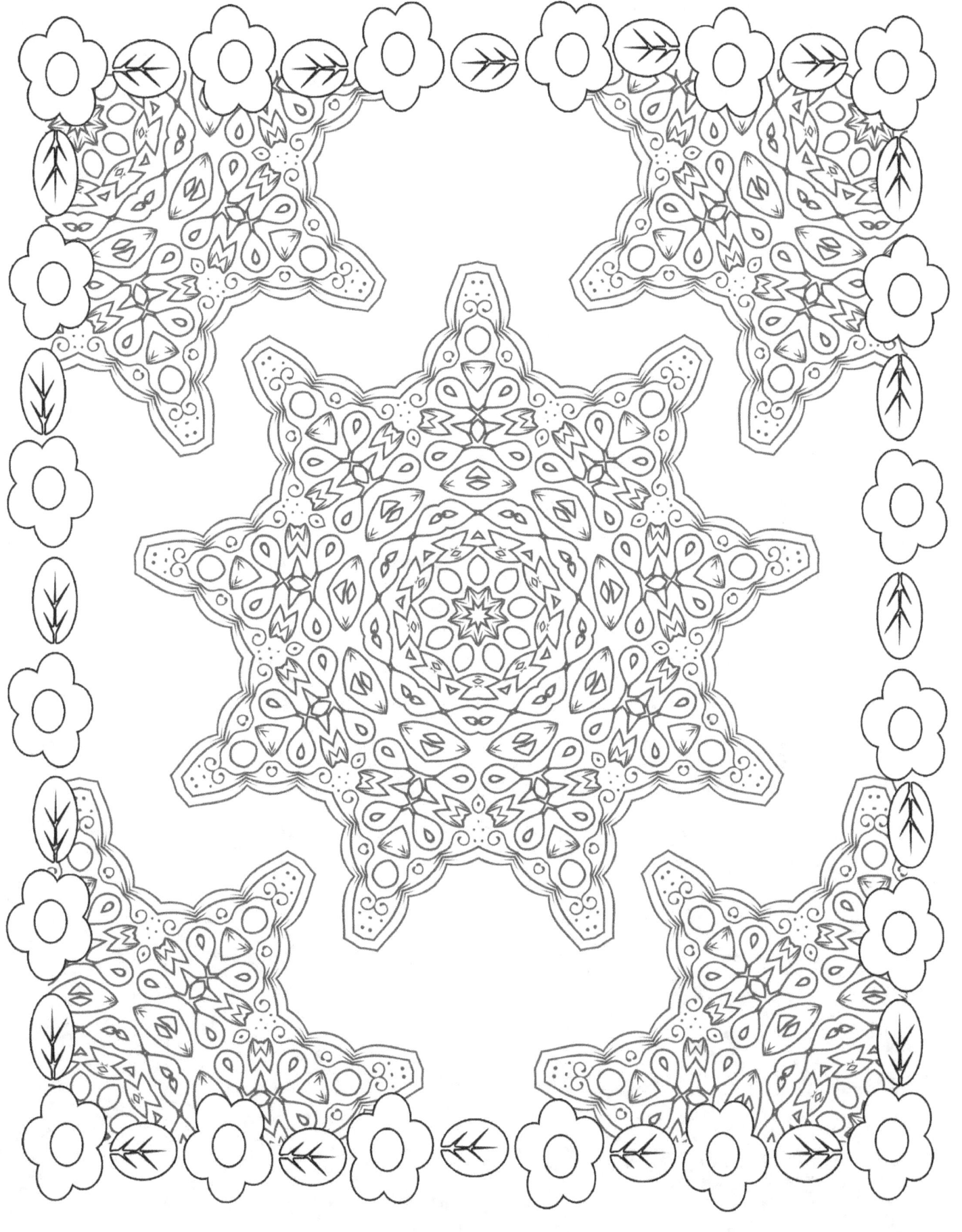

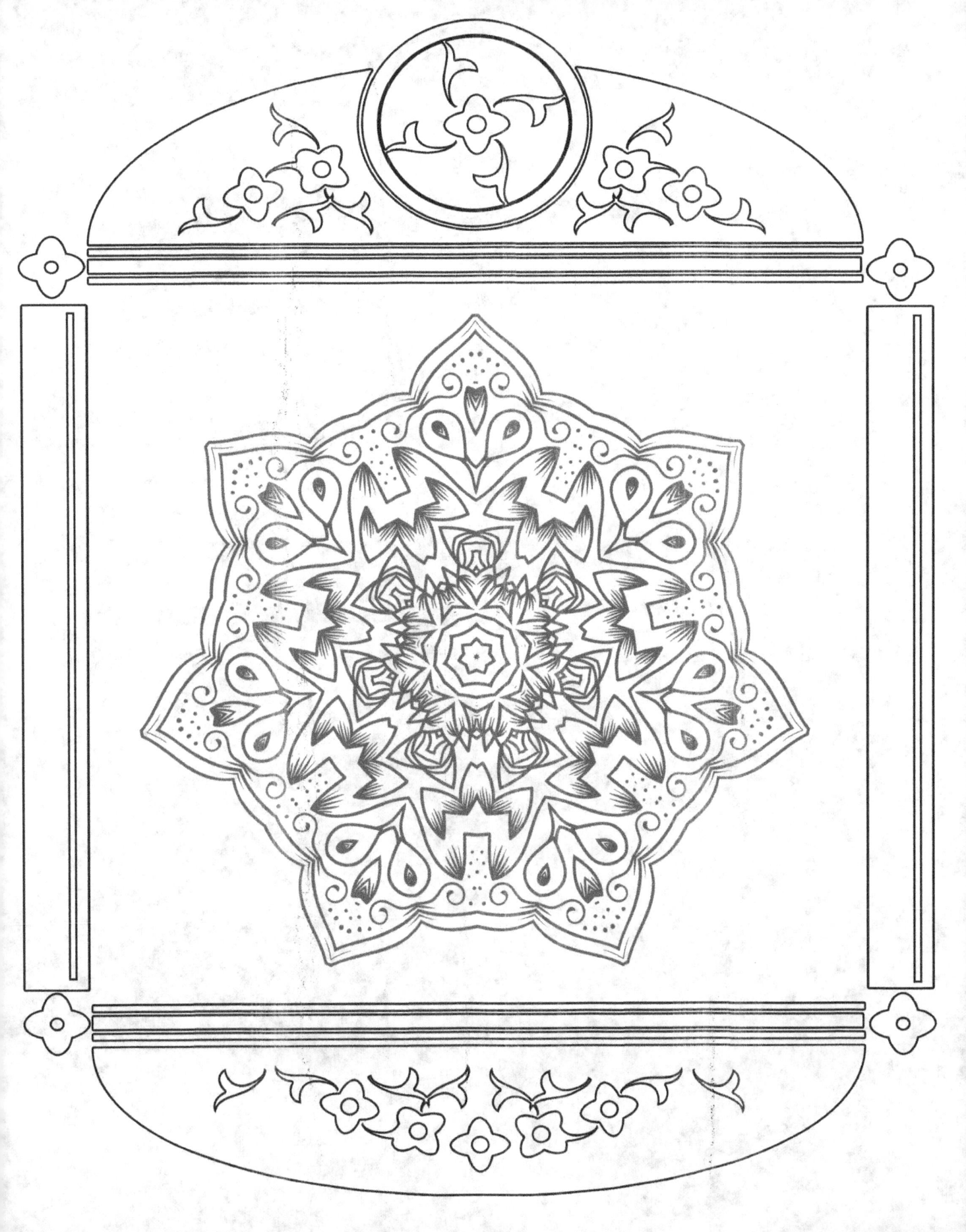

WHERE wisdom reigns, THERE is no
conflict between Thinking and FEELing

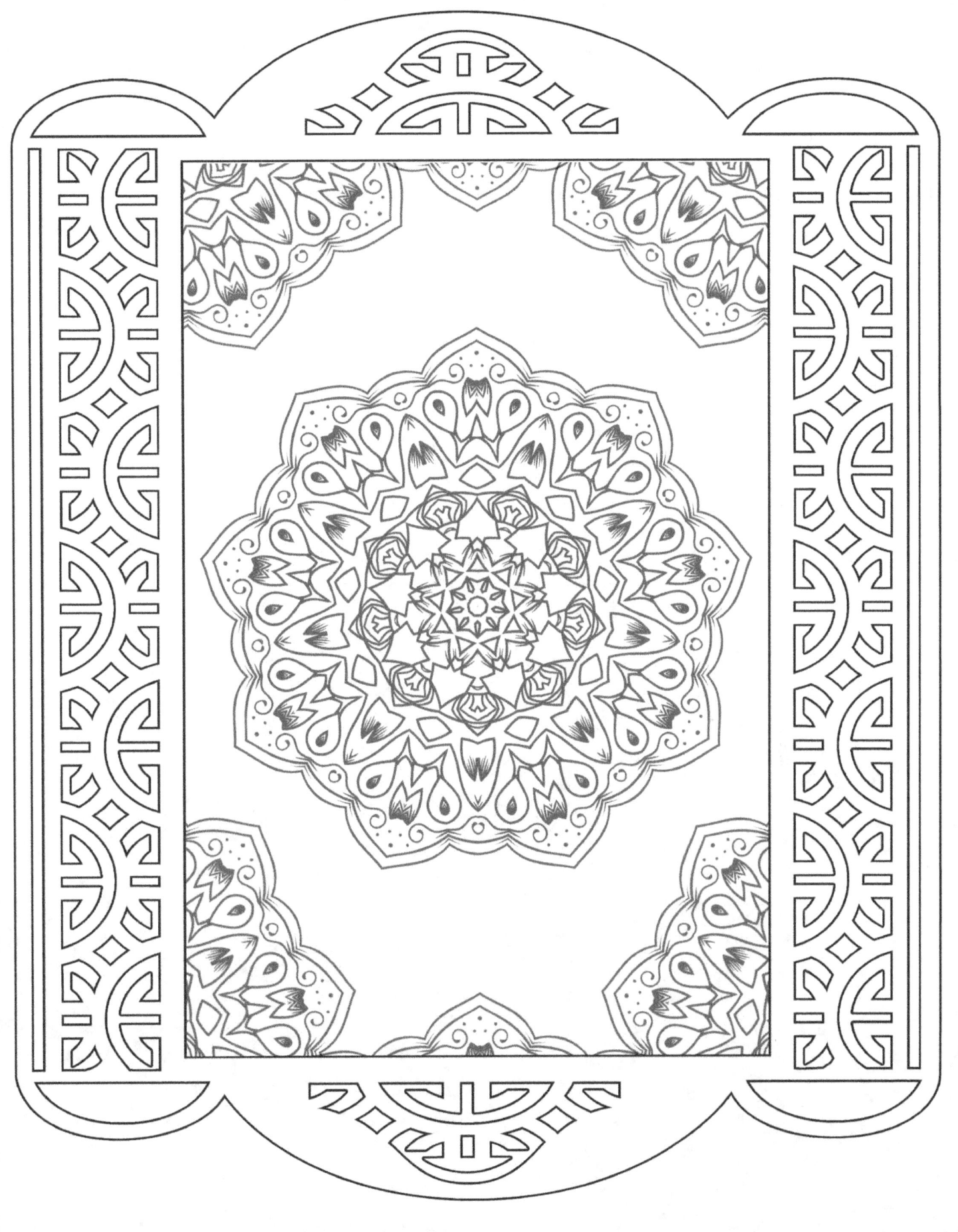

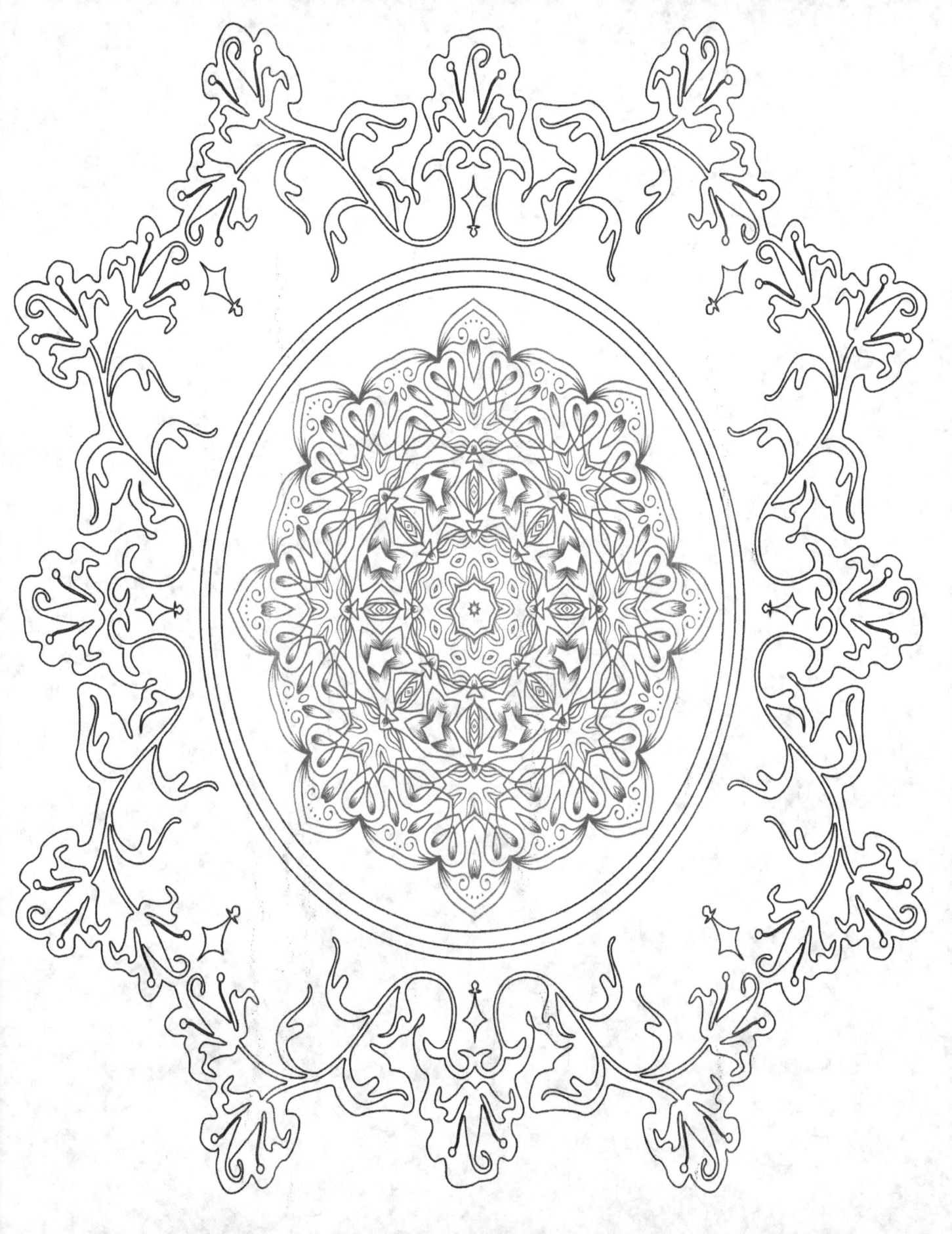

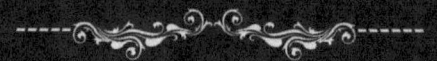

THE GREATEST TRAGEDY OF THE FAMILY IS
THE UNLIVED LIVES OF THE PARENTS

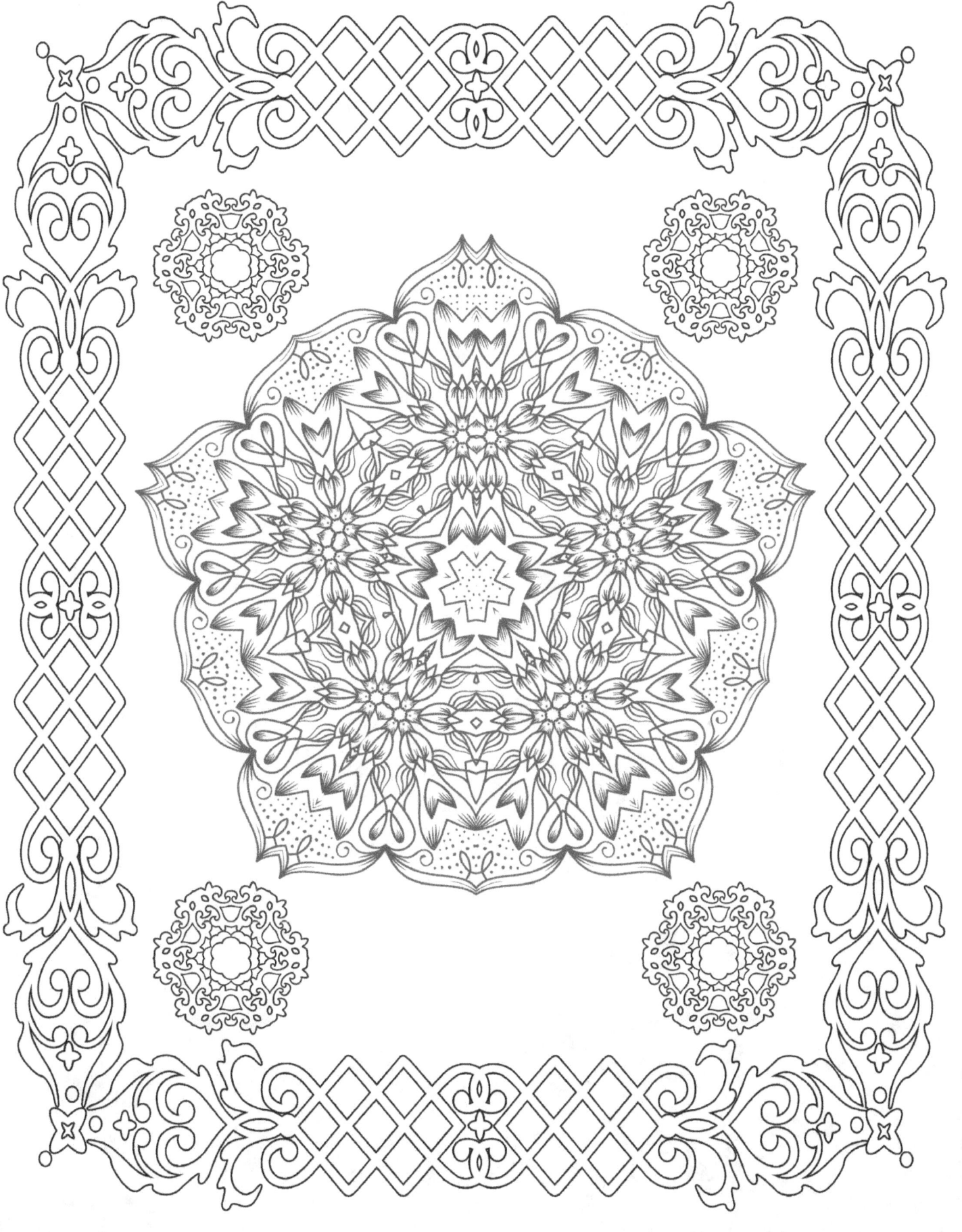

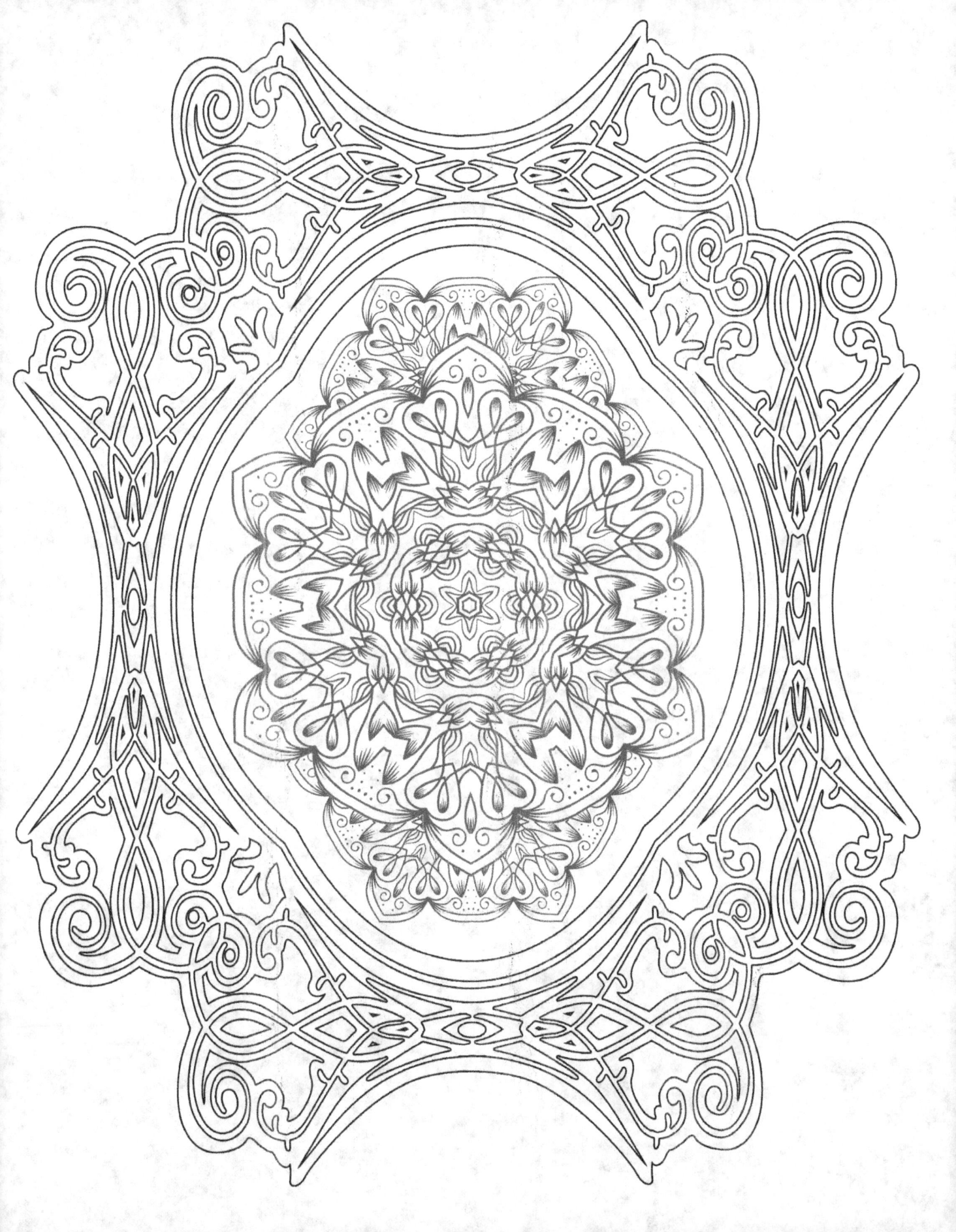

WE CANNOT CHANGE ANYTHING UNLESS WE ACCEPT IT...

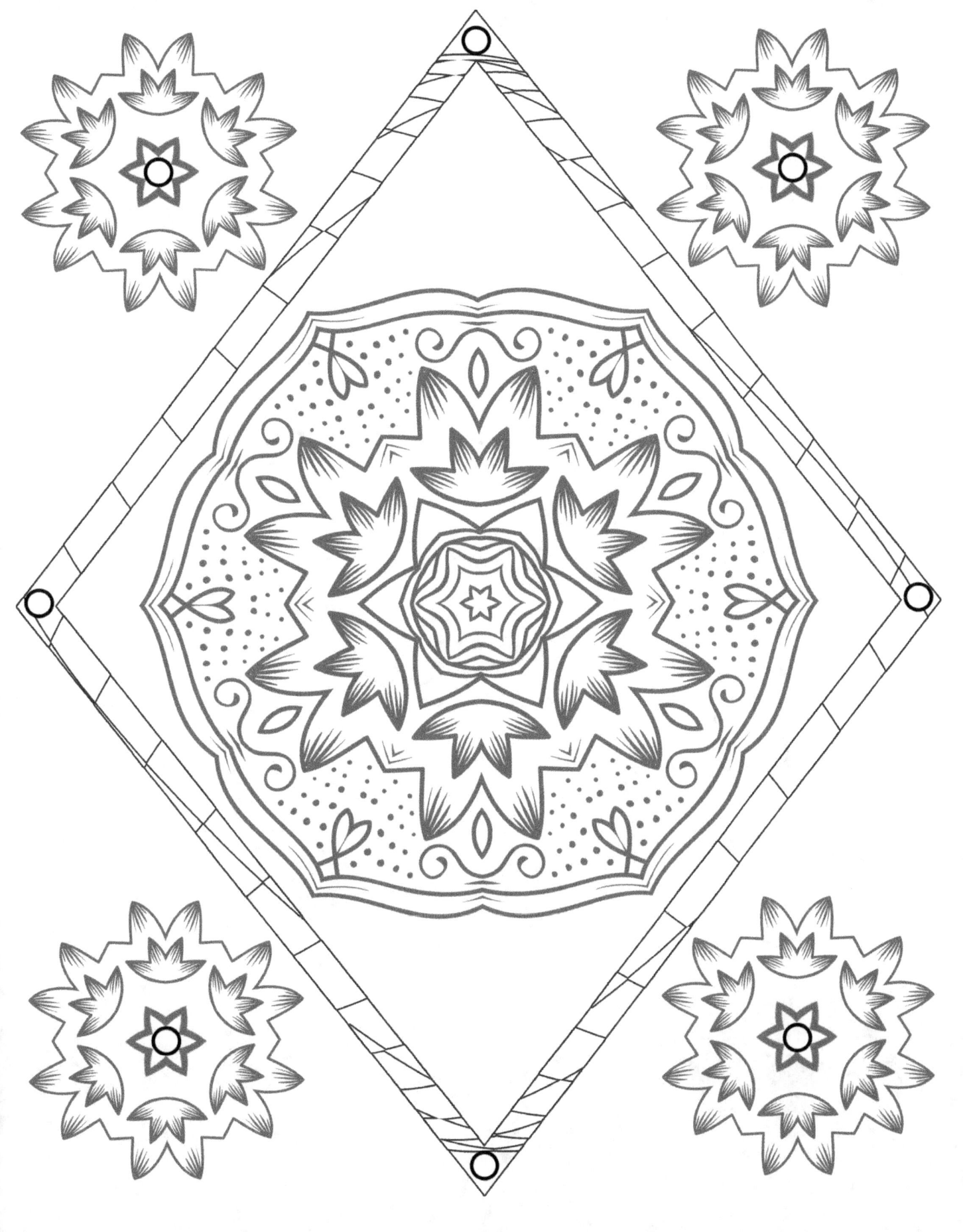

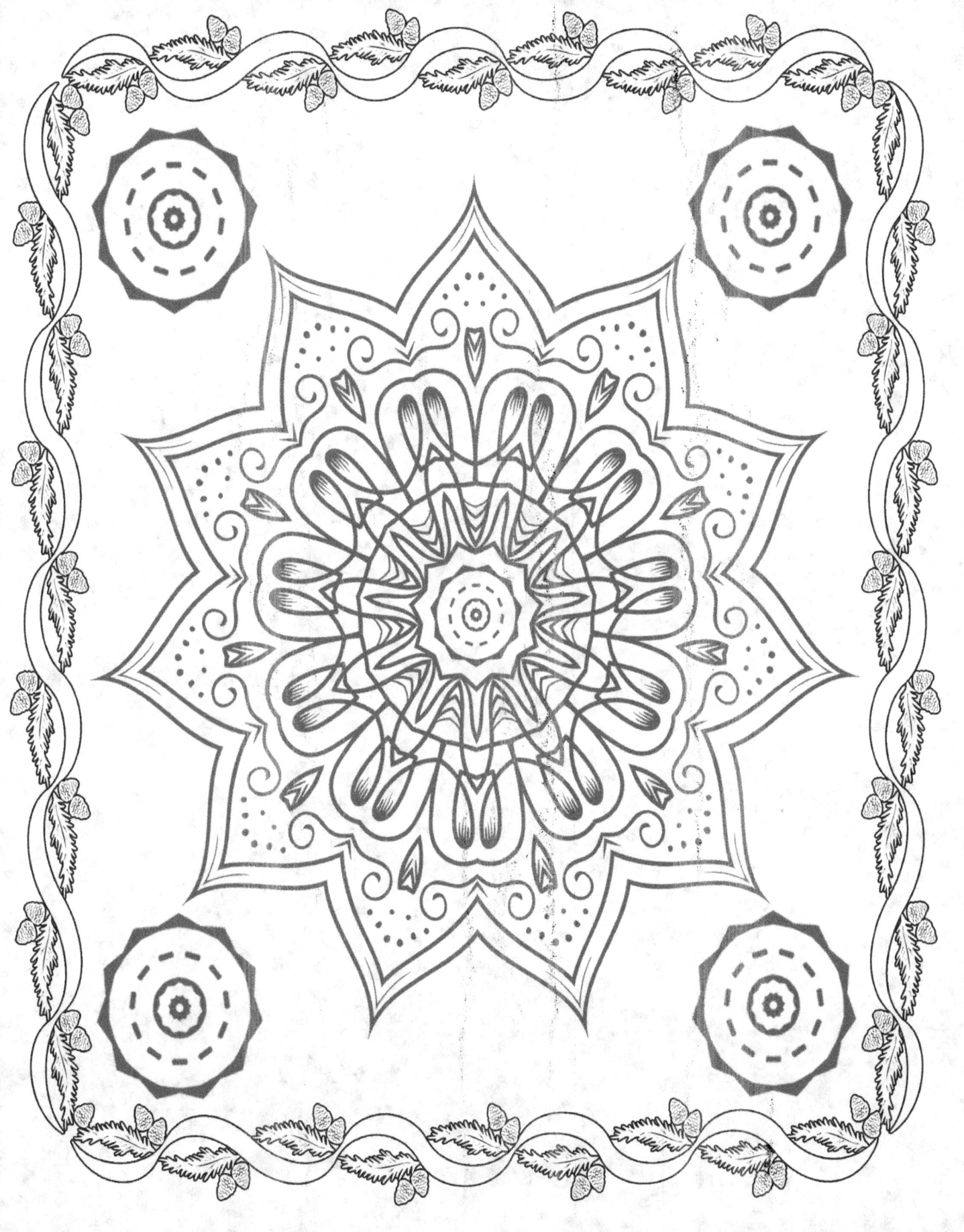

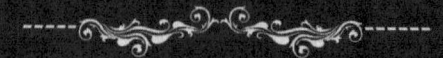

THE SHOE THAT FITS ONE PERSON PINCHES ANOTHER;
THERE IS NO RECIPE FOR LIVING THAT SUITS ALL CASES

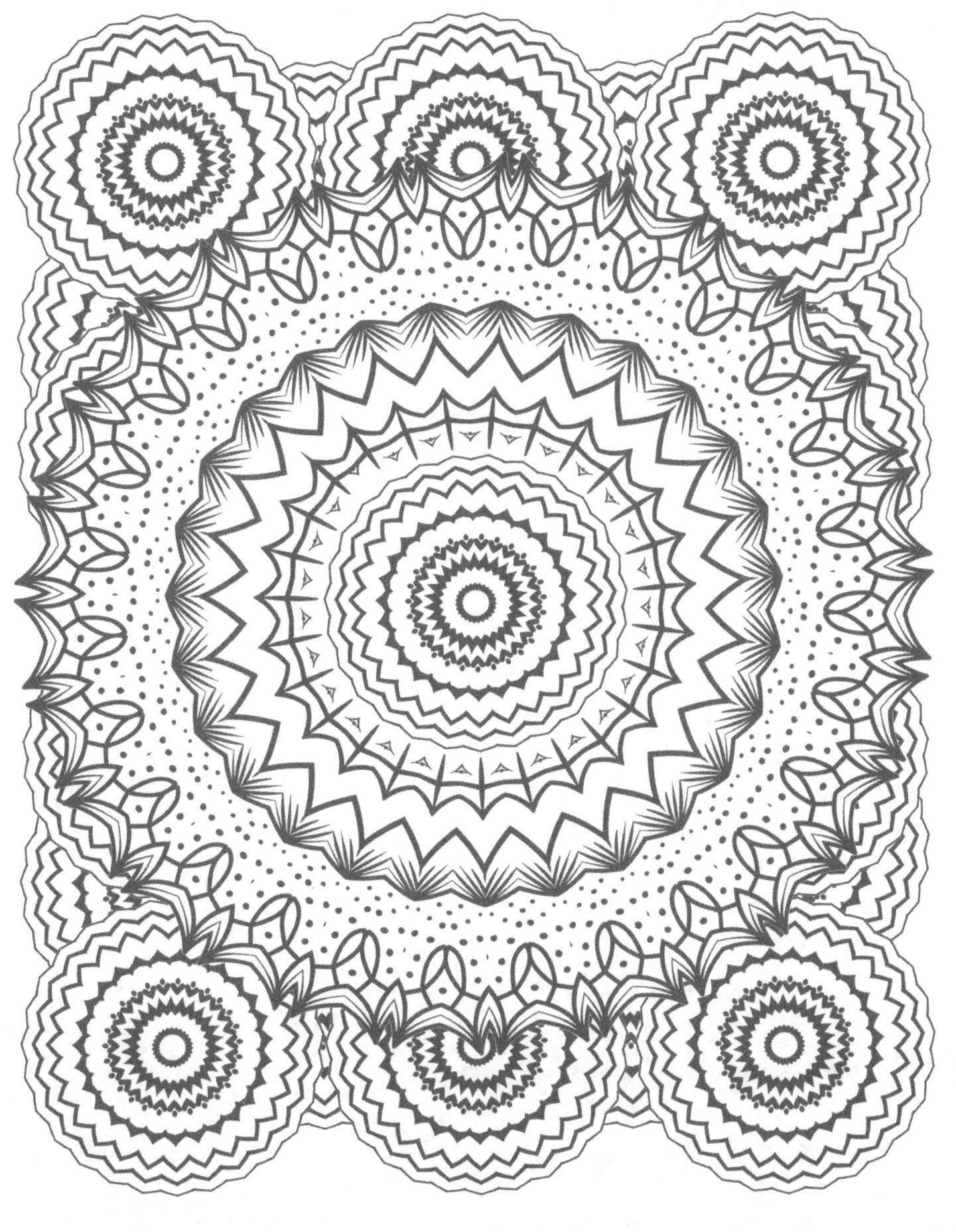

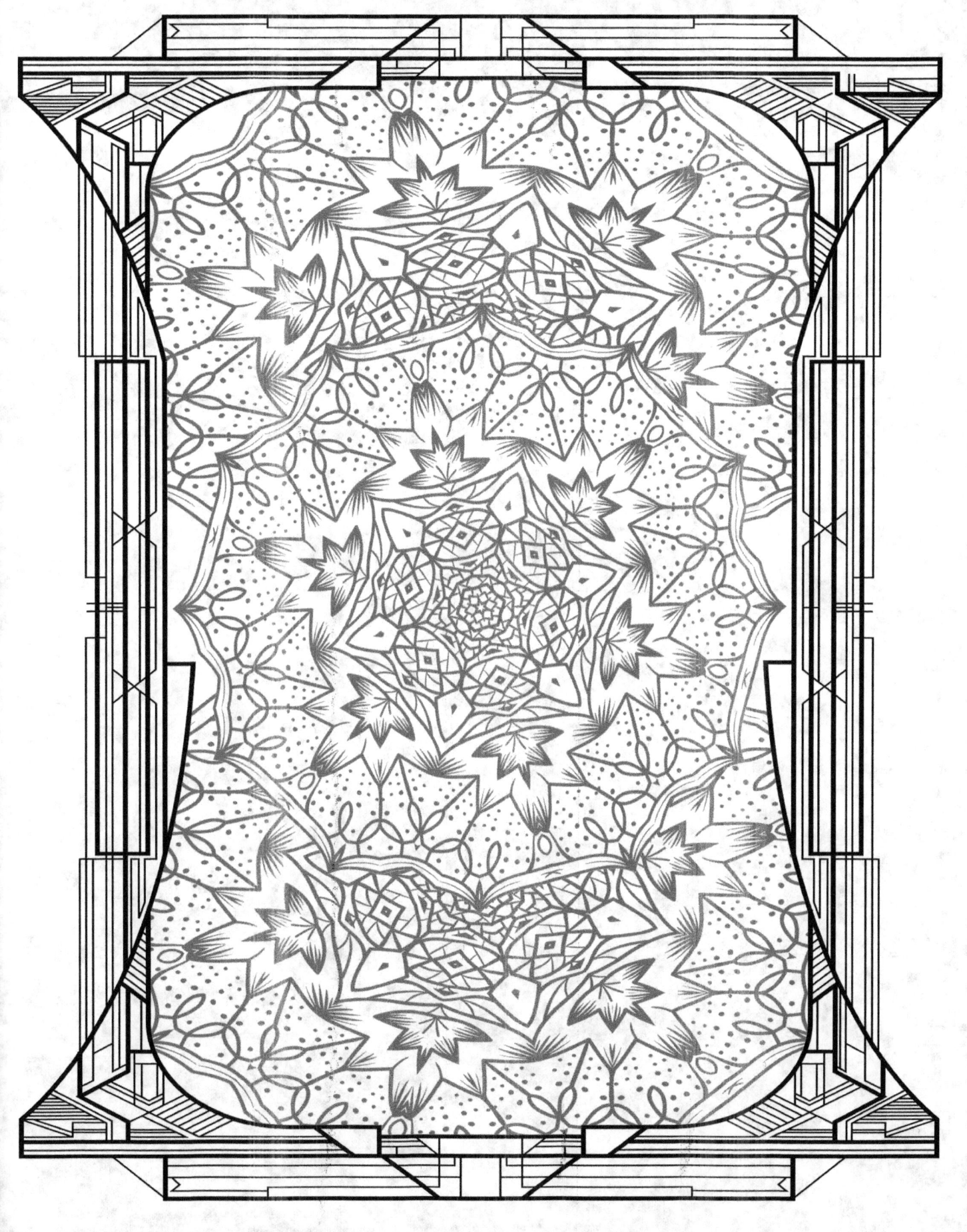

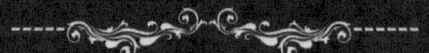

MISTAKES ARE, AFTER ALL, THE FOUNDATIONS OF TRUTH,

AND IF A MAN DOES NOT KNOW WHAT A THING IS,

IT IS AT LEAST AN INCREASE IN KNOWLEDGE

IF HE KNOWS WHAT IT IS NOT

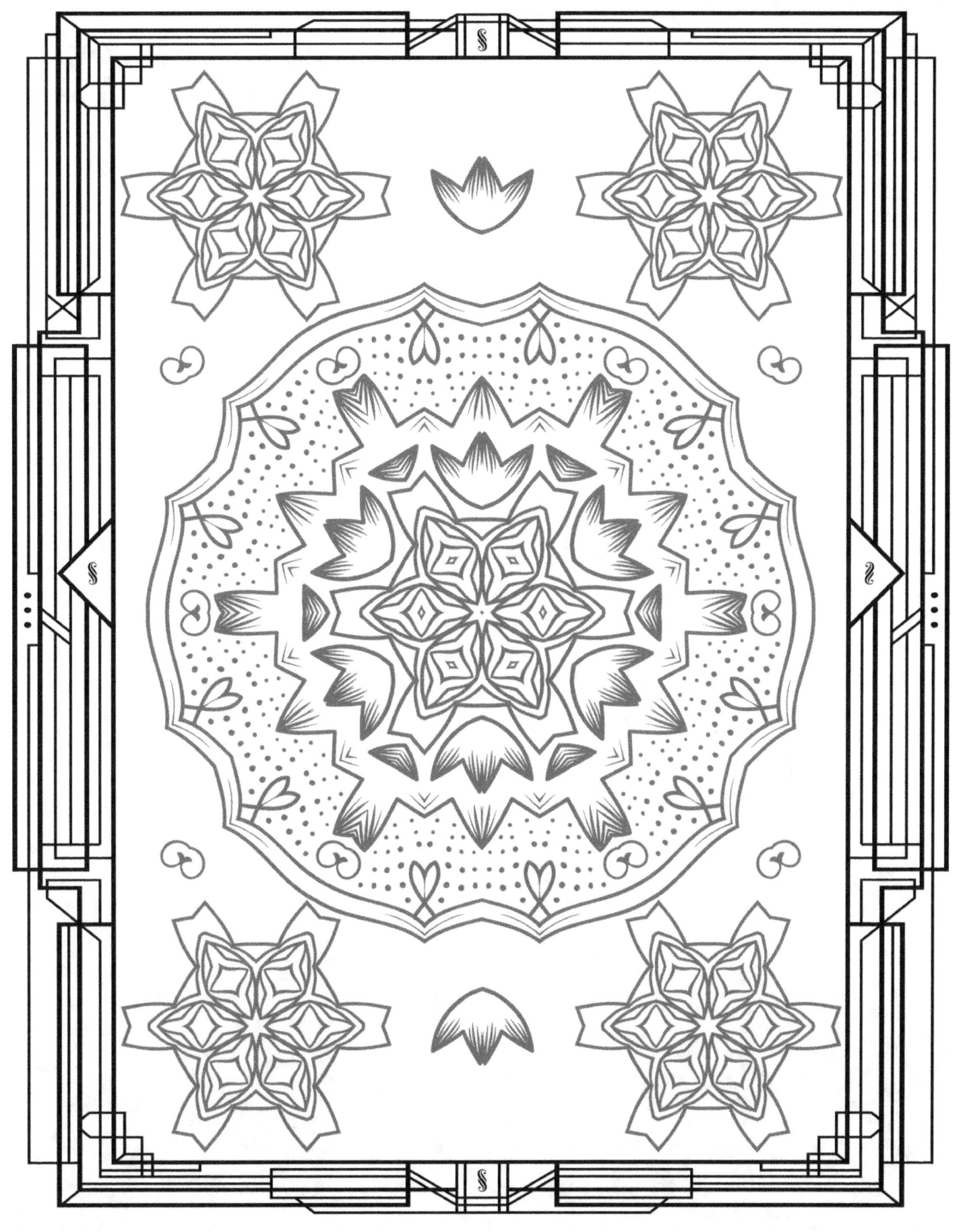

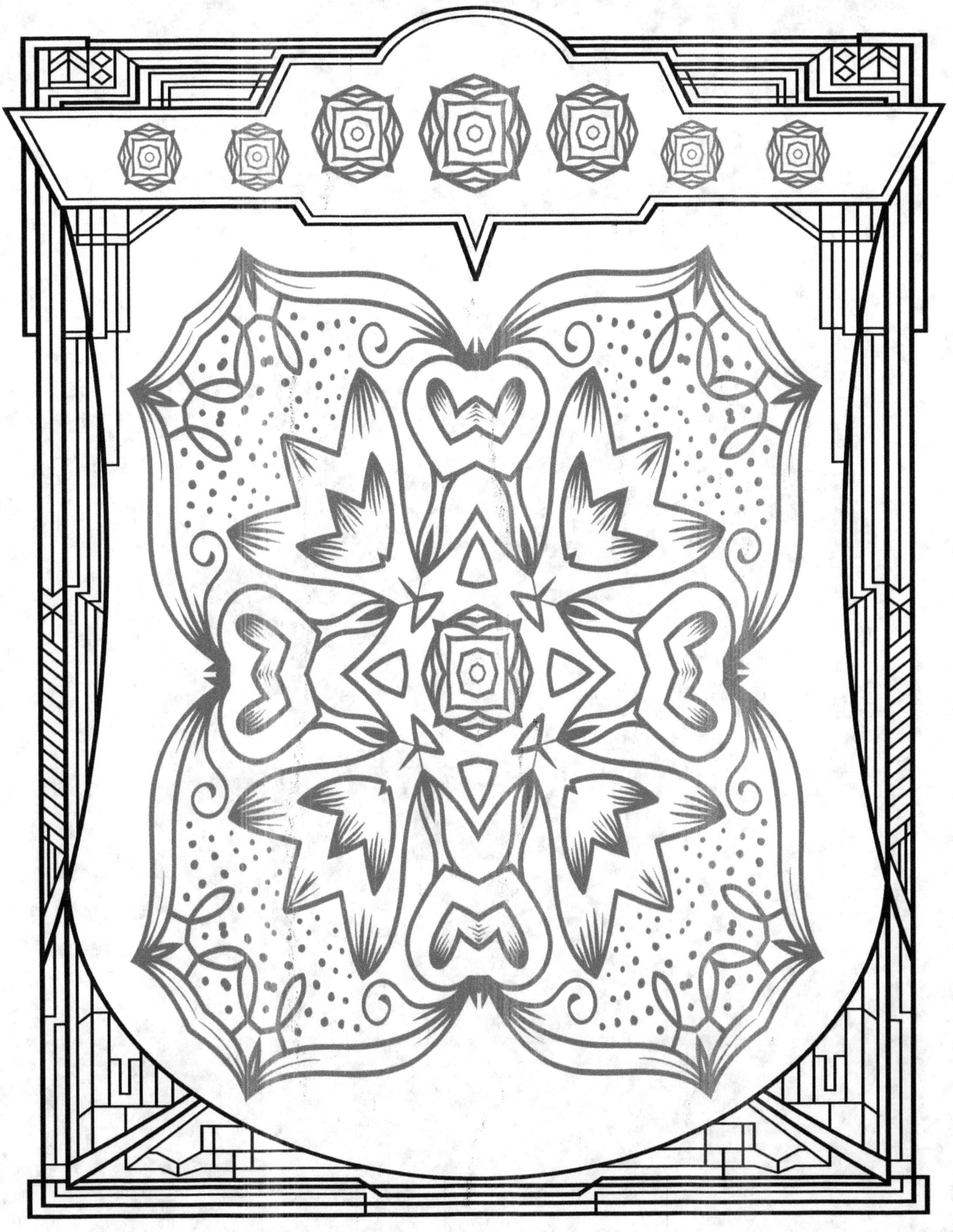

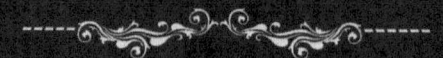

Every form of addiction is bad,
no matter whether the narcotic be
alcohol, morphine or idealism

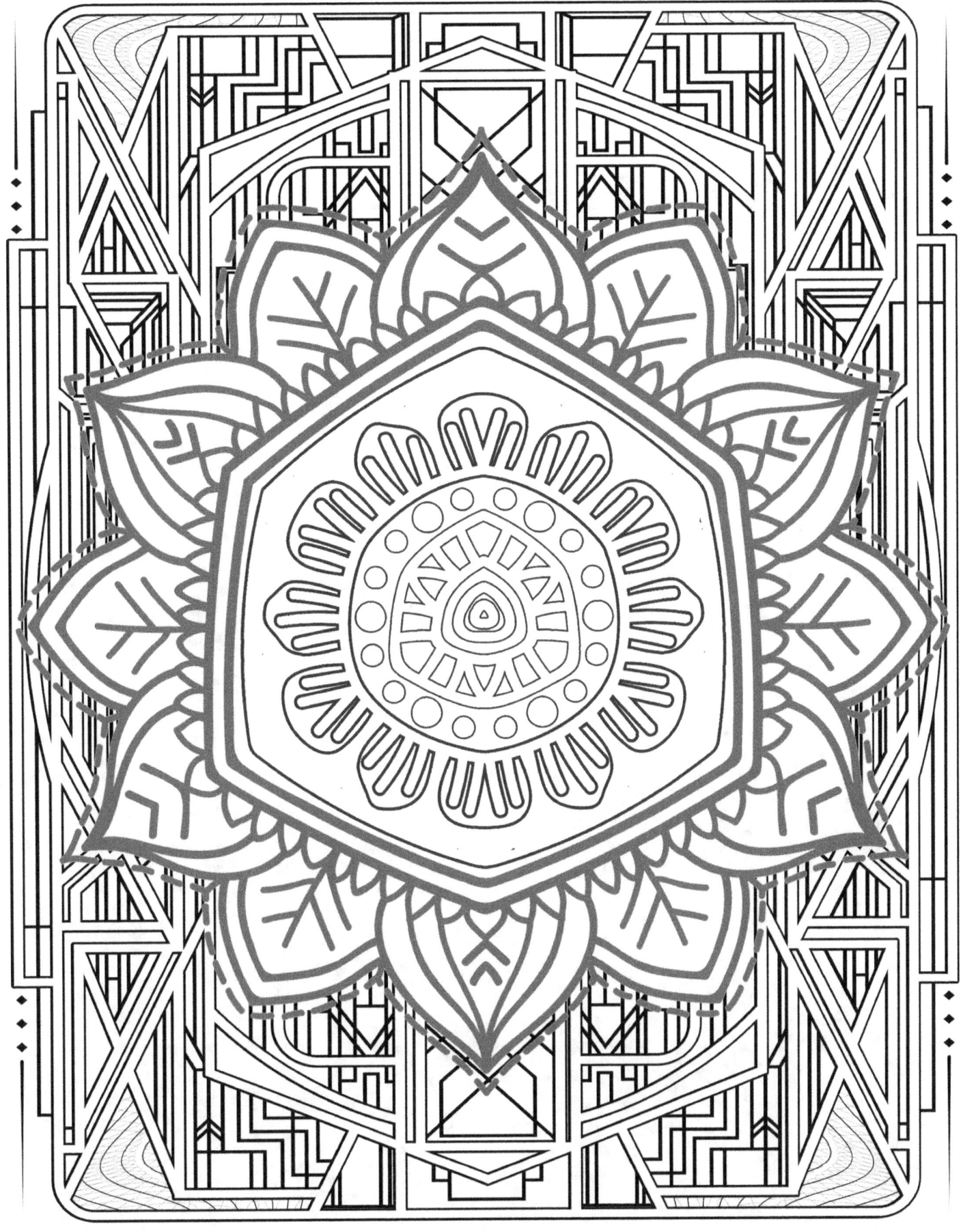

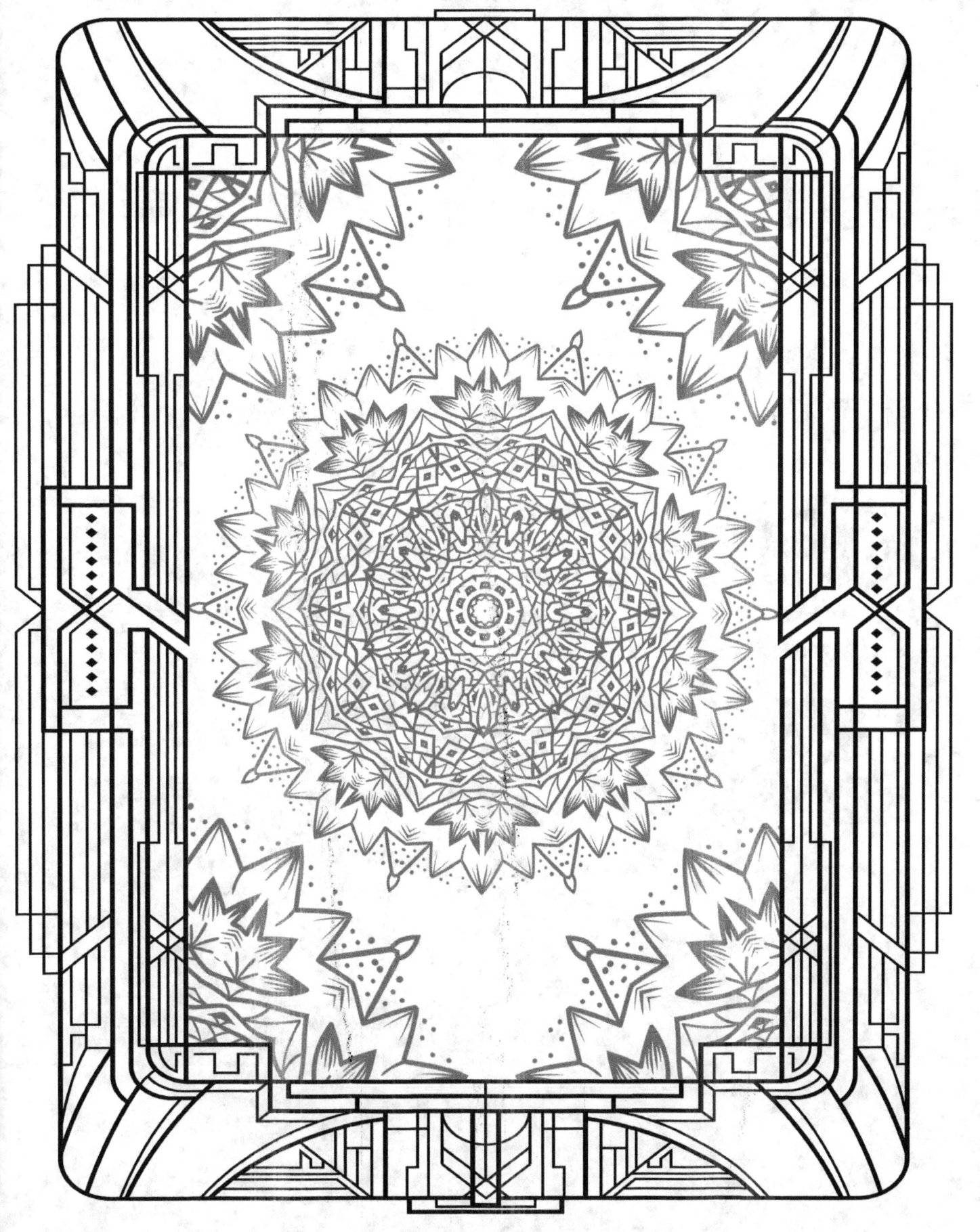

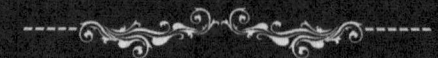

Your visions will become clear only when
you can look into your own heart.
Who looks outside, dreams; who looks inside, awakes

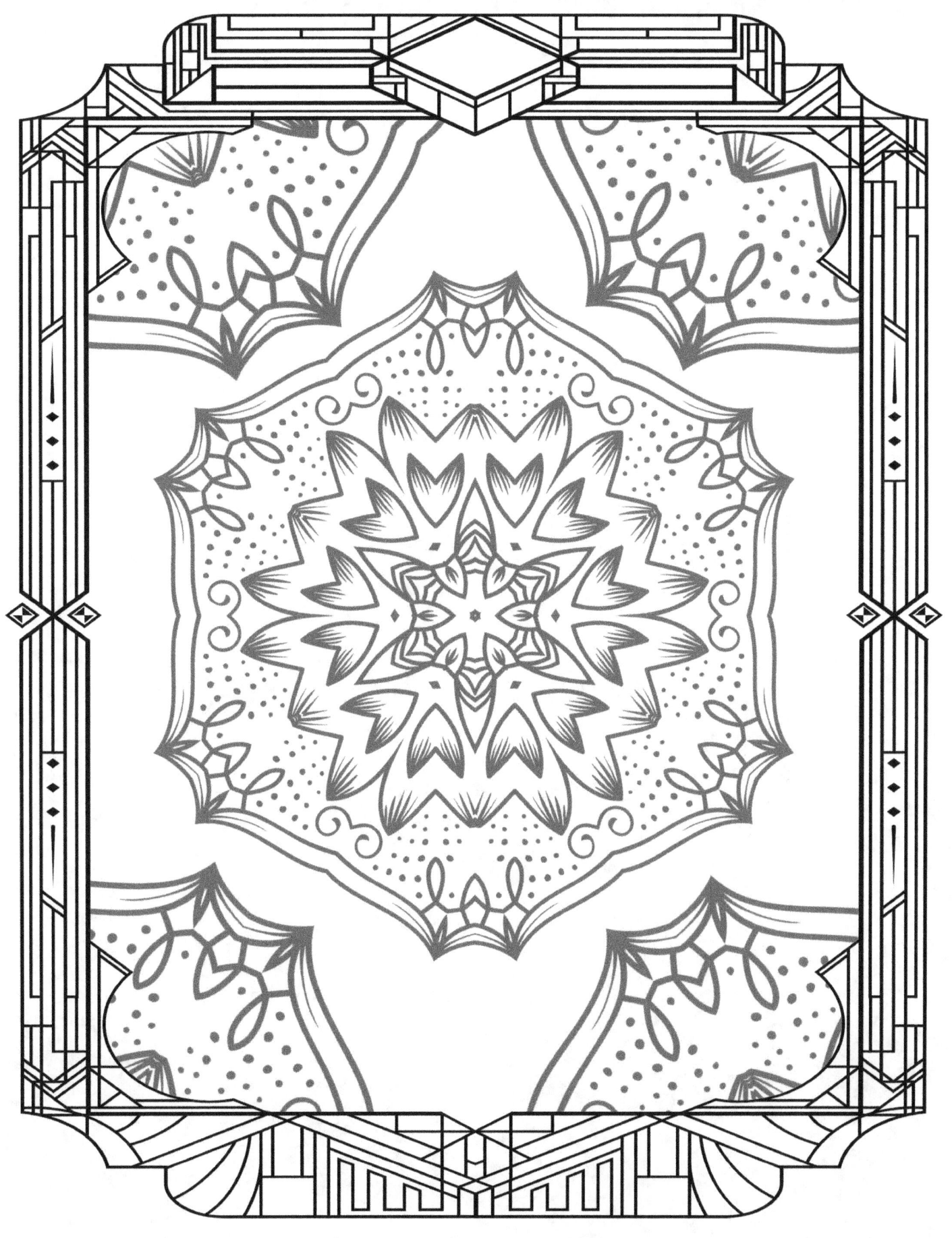

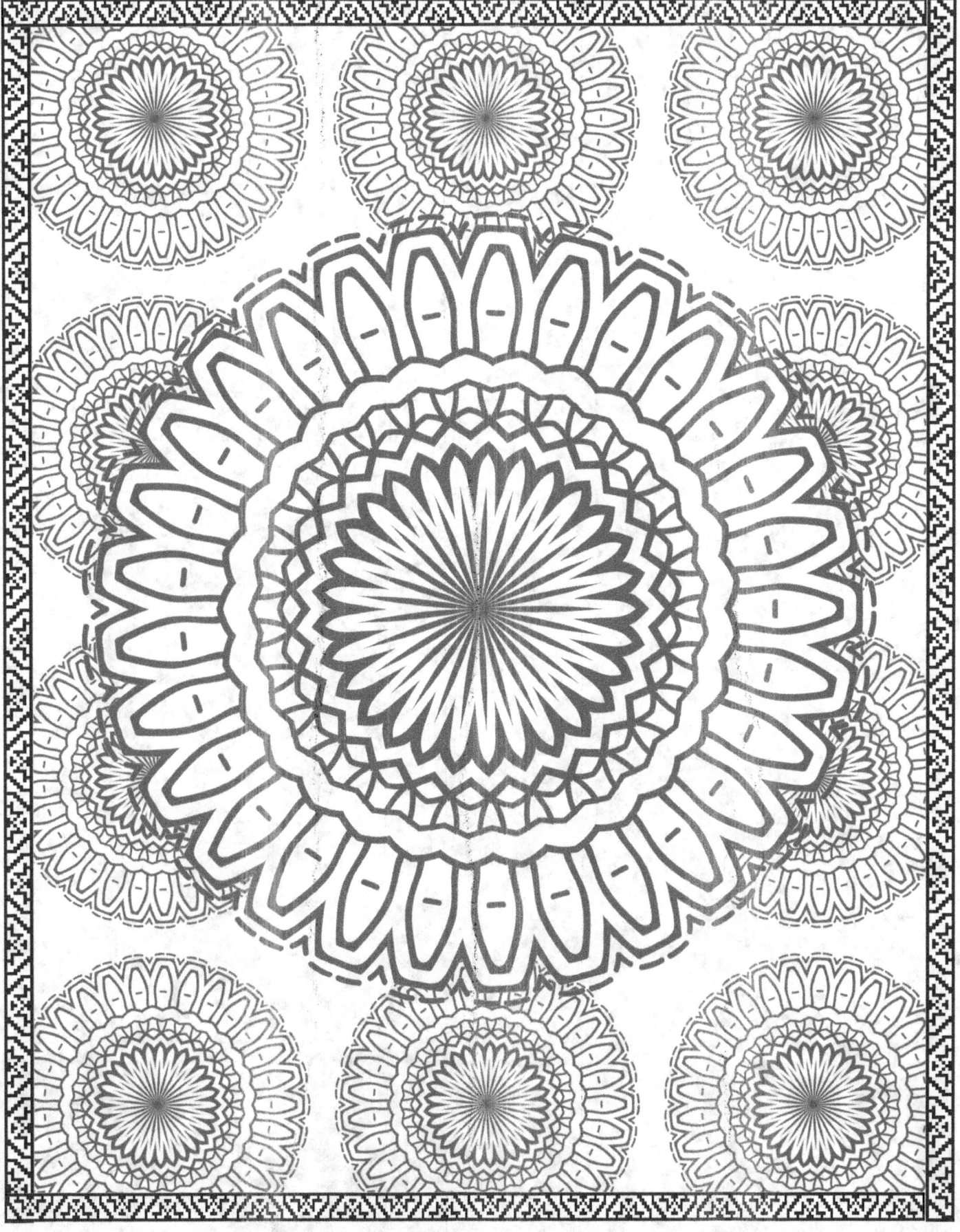

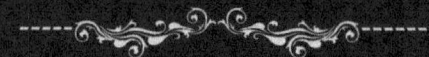

THE MEETING OF TWO PERSONALITIES IS LIKE
THE CONTACT OF TWO CHEMICAL SUBSTANCES:
IF THERE IS ANY REACTION, BOTH ARE TRANSFORMED

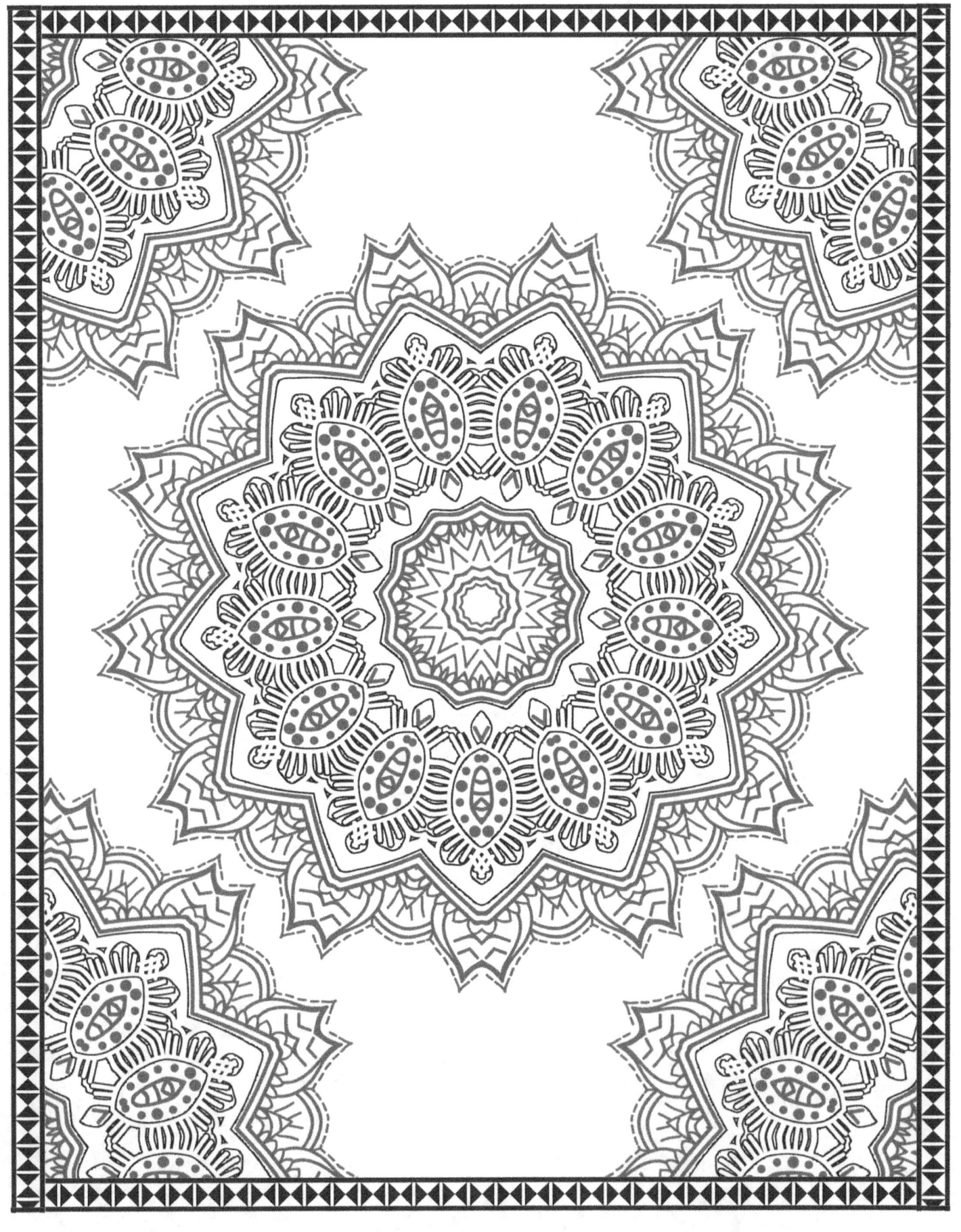

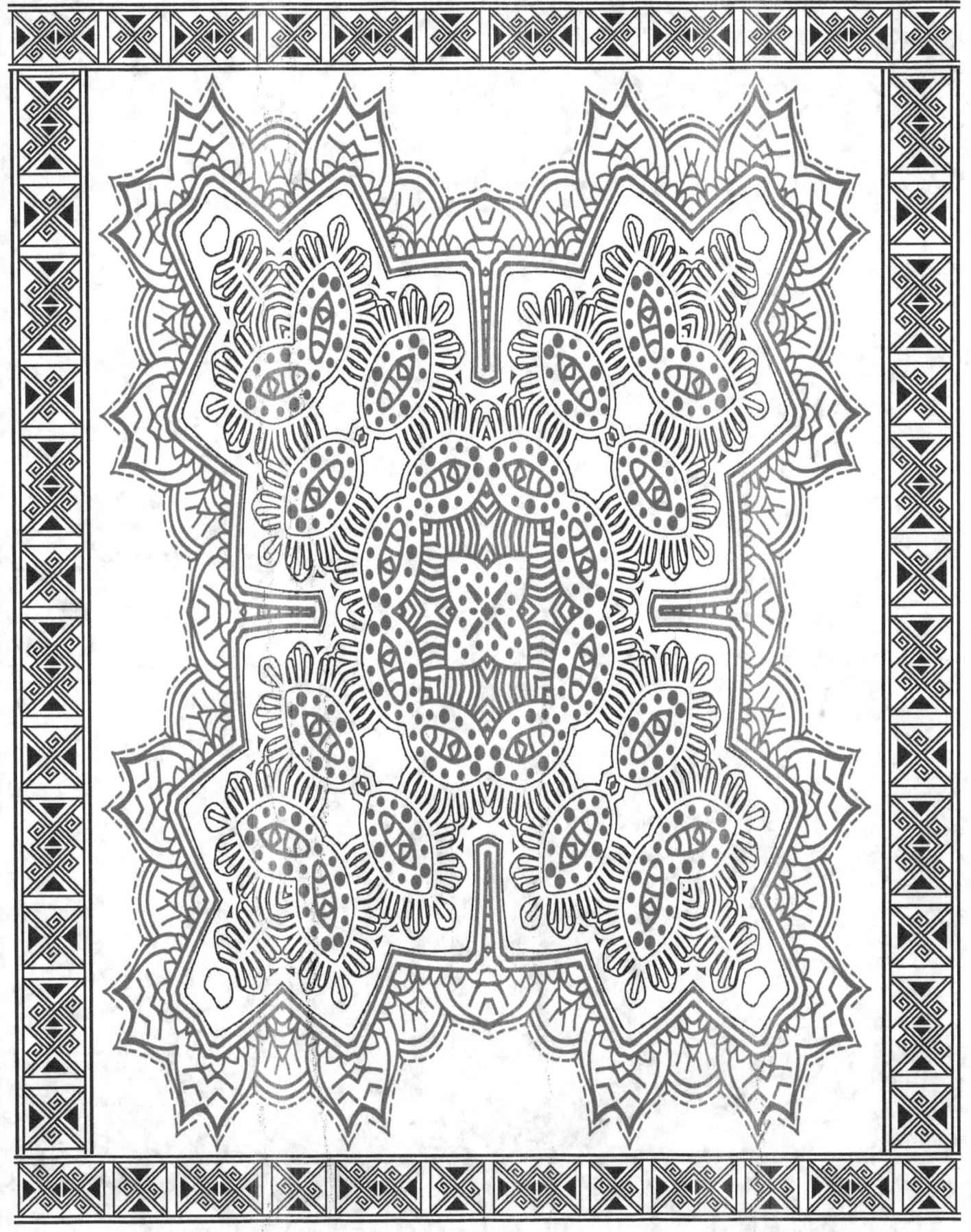

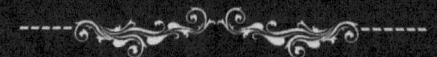

THE LEAST OF THINGS WITH A MEANING

IS WORTH MORE IN LIFE THAN THE

GREATEST OF THINGS WITHOUT IT

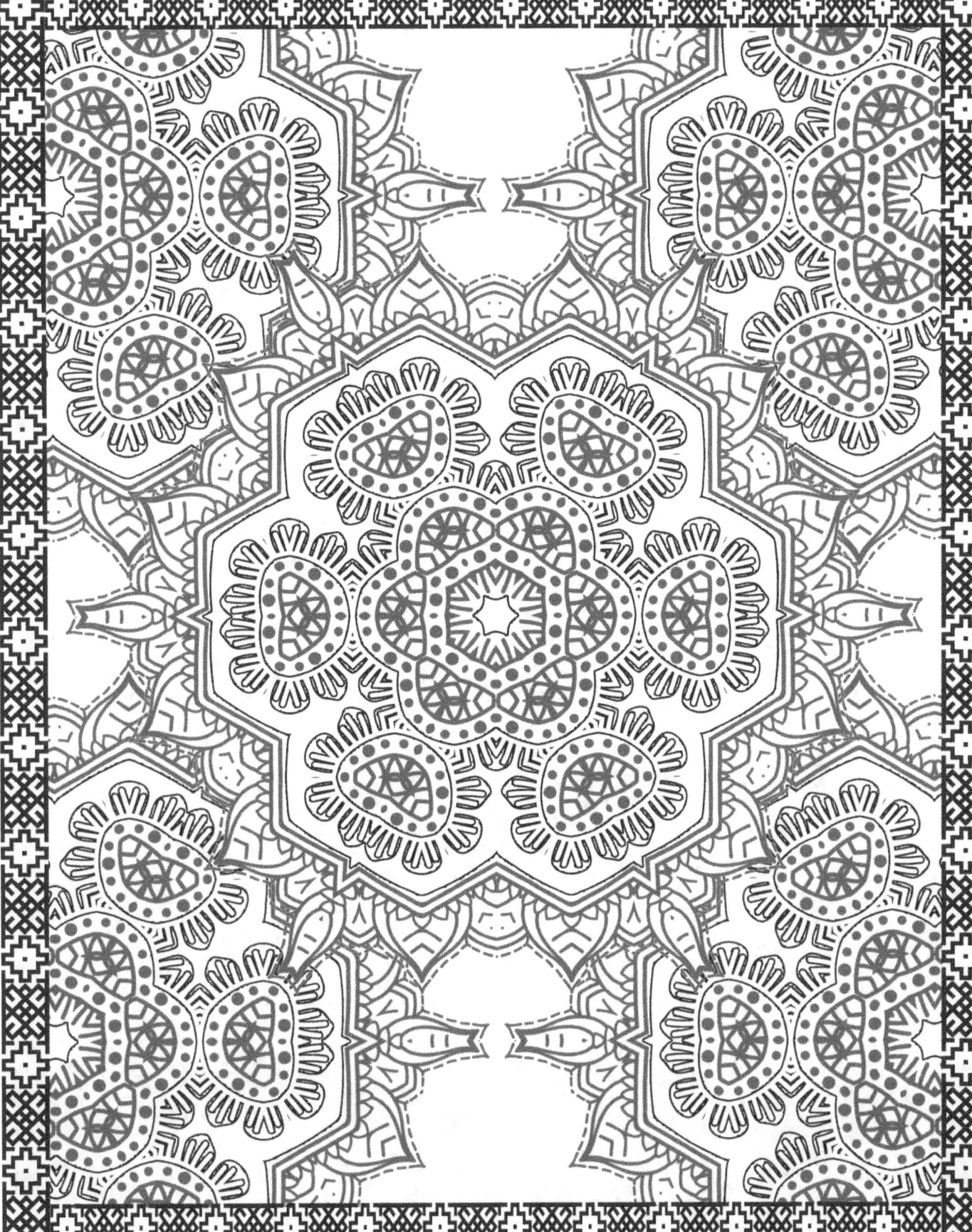

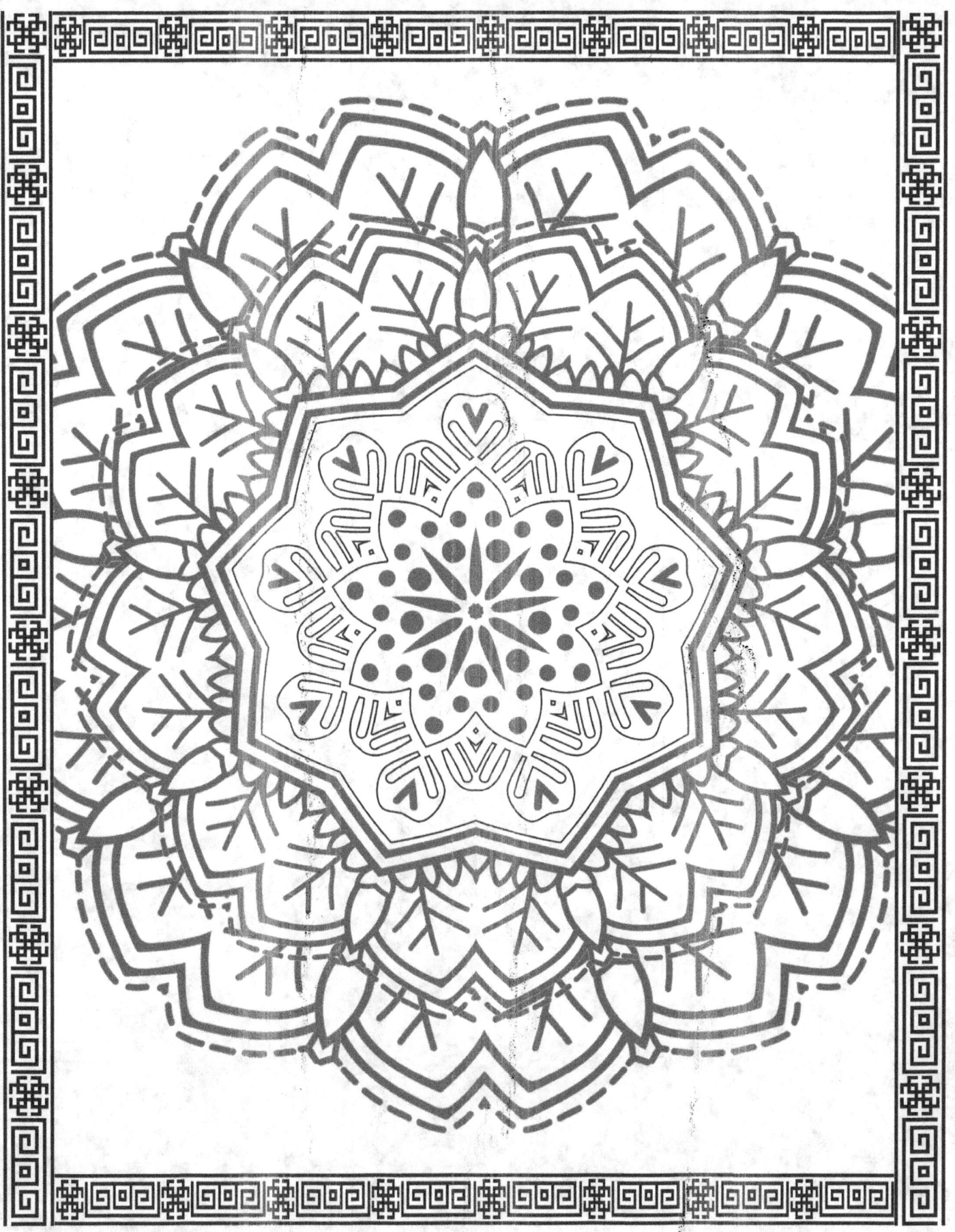

MAN NEEDS difficulties;
THEY ARE NECESSARY FOR HEALTH...

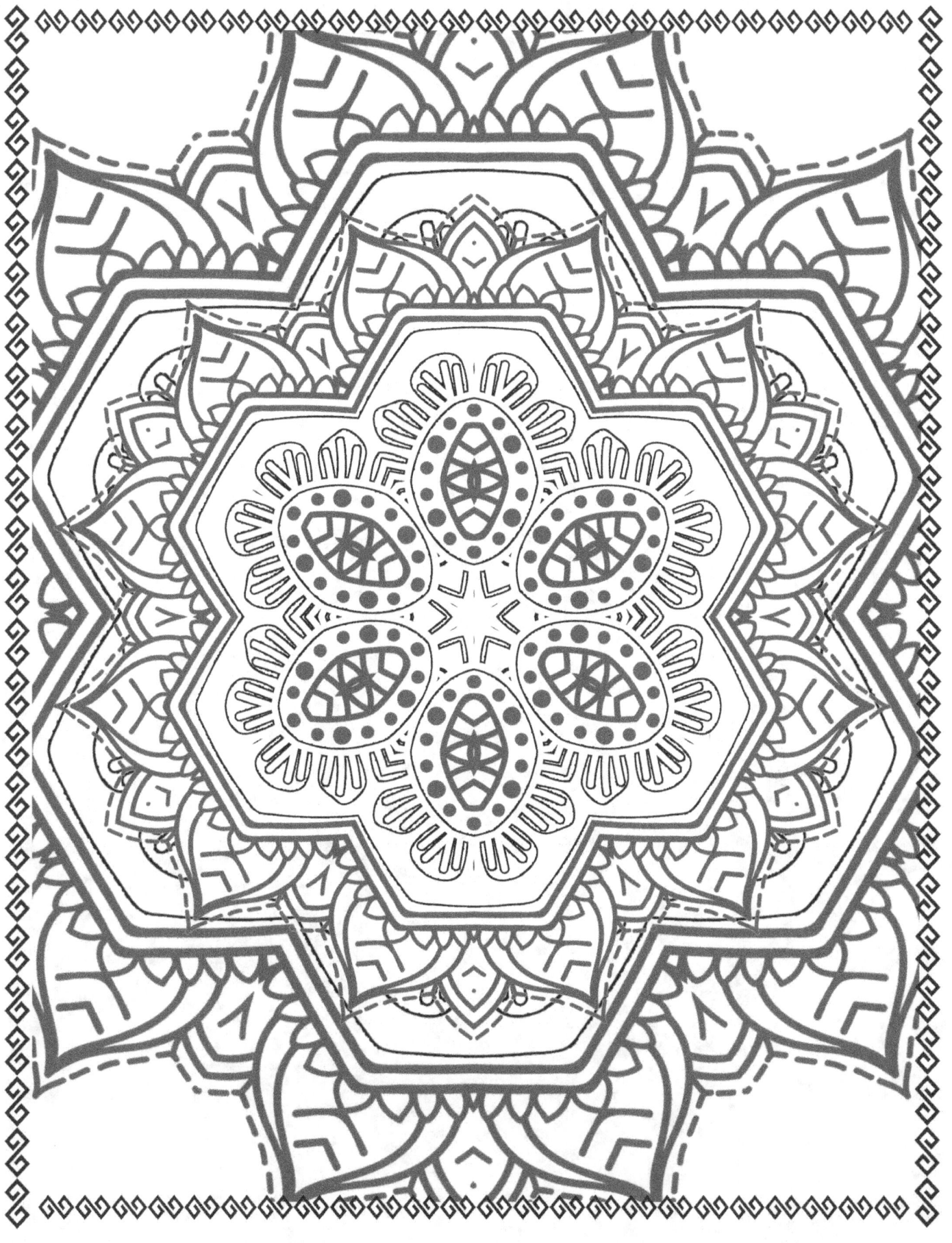

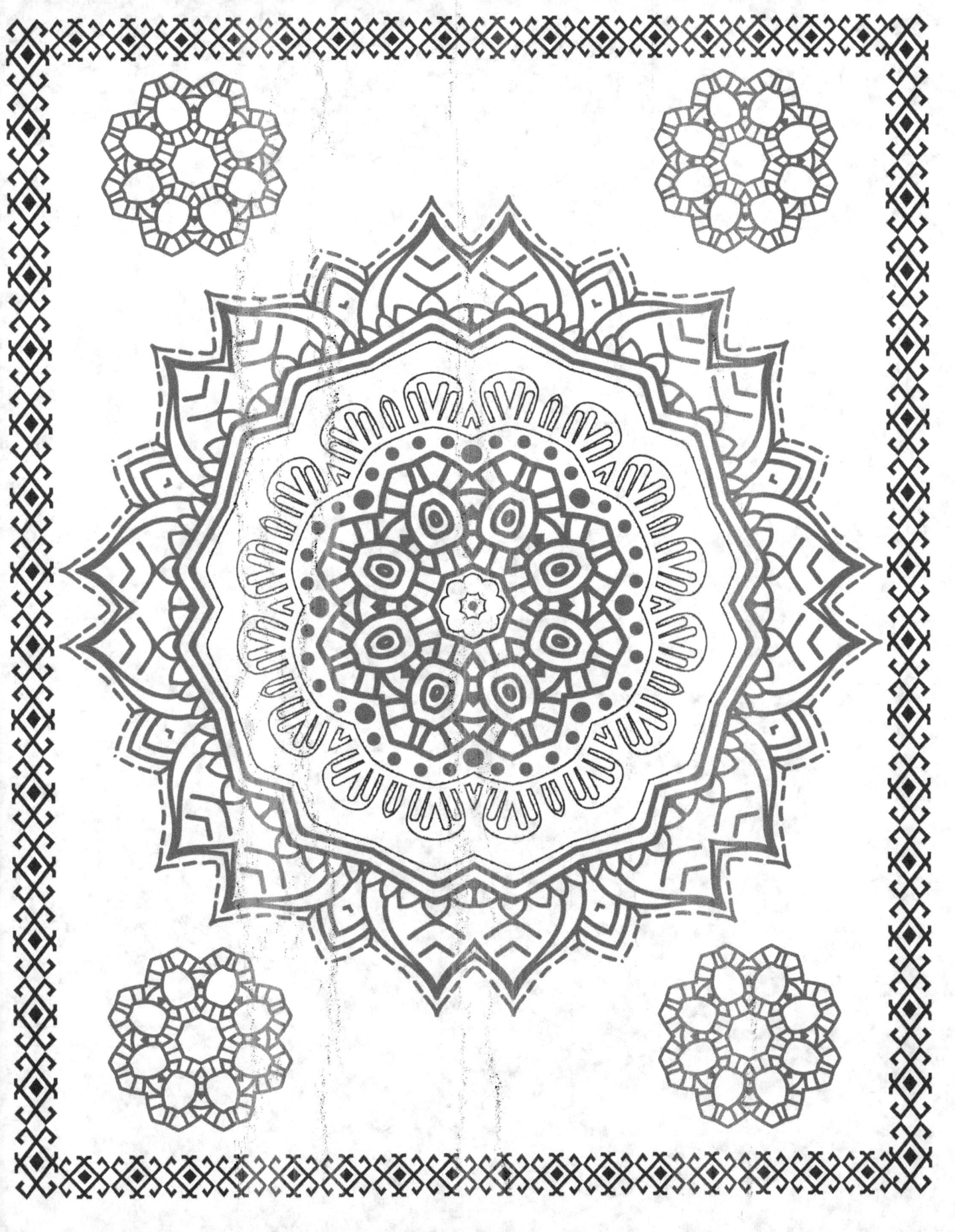

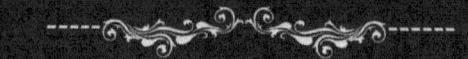

WITHOUT FREEDOM THERE CAN BE NO MORALITY

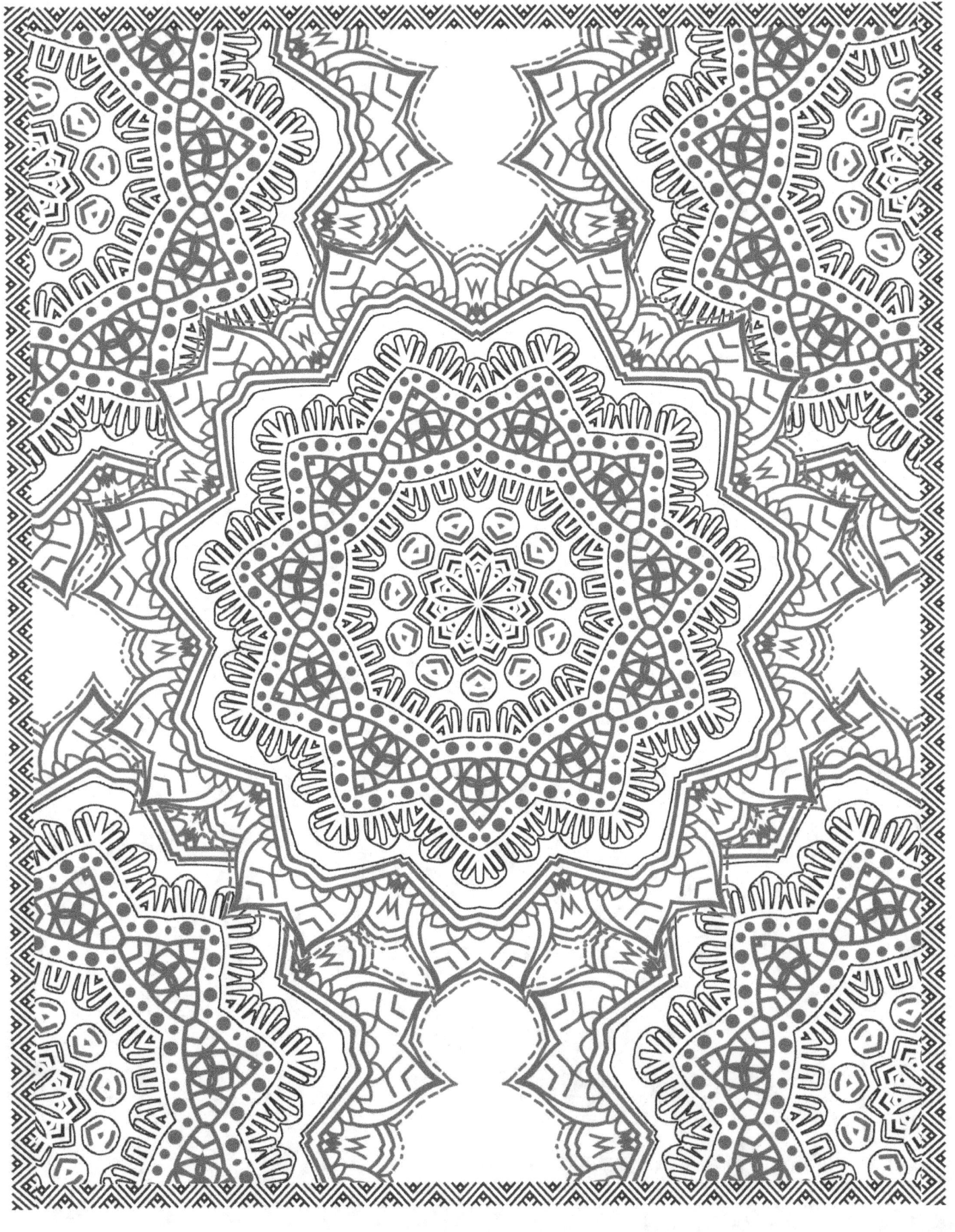

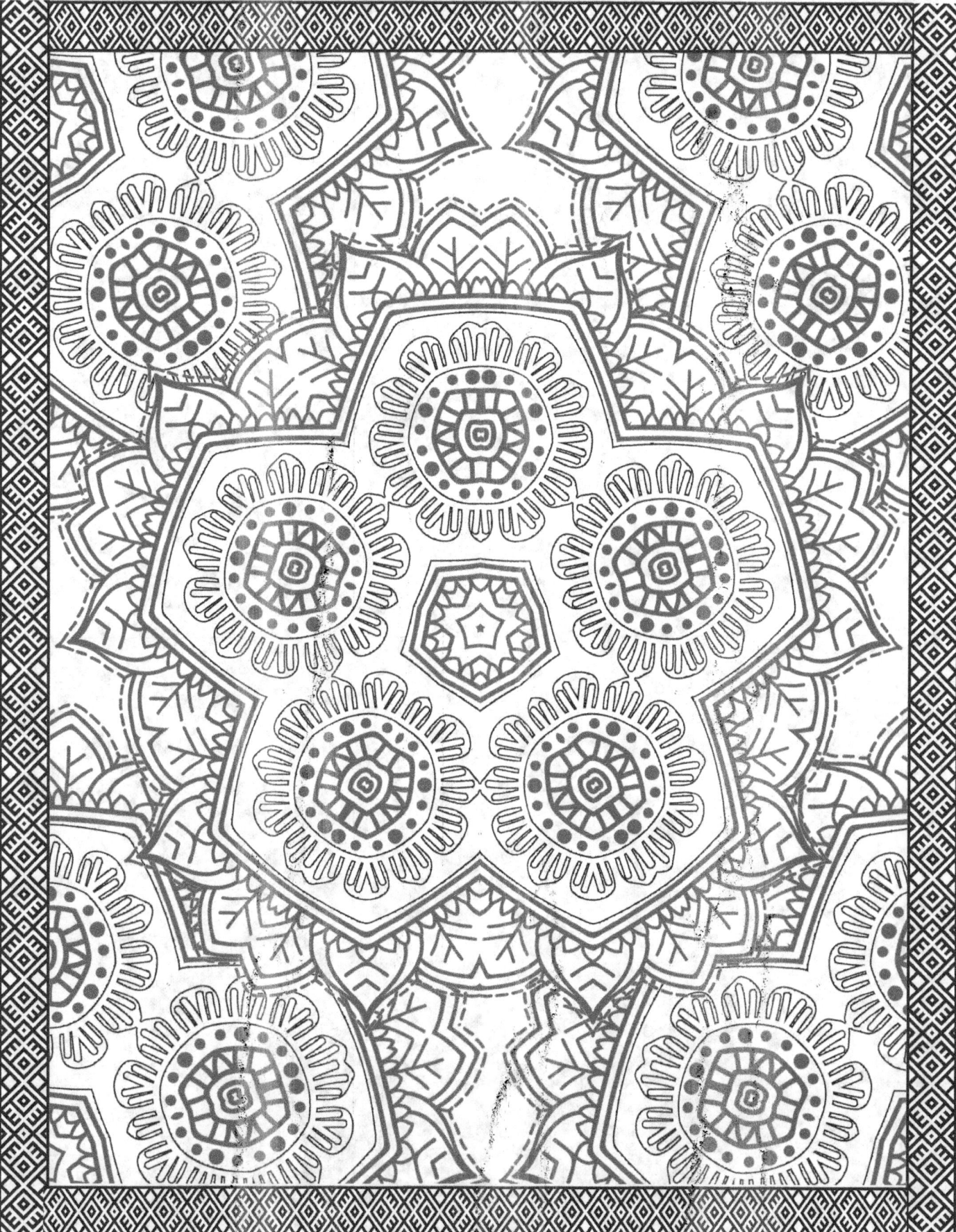

ENVY doES NoT Allow HUMANITY To SlEEp...

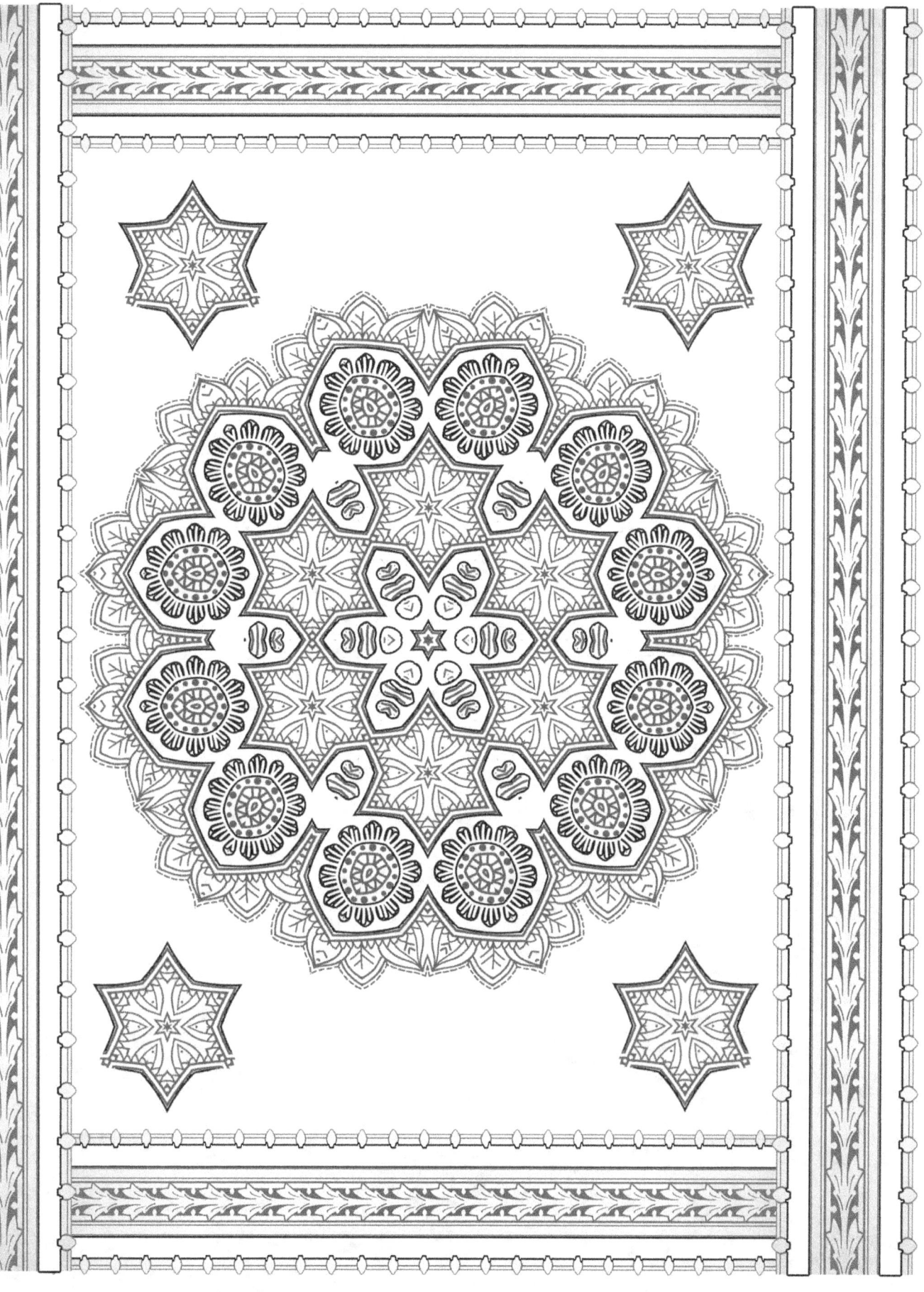

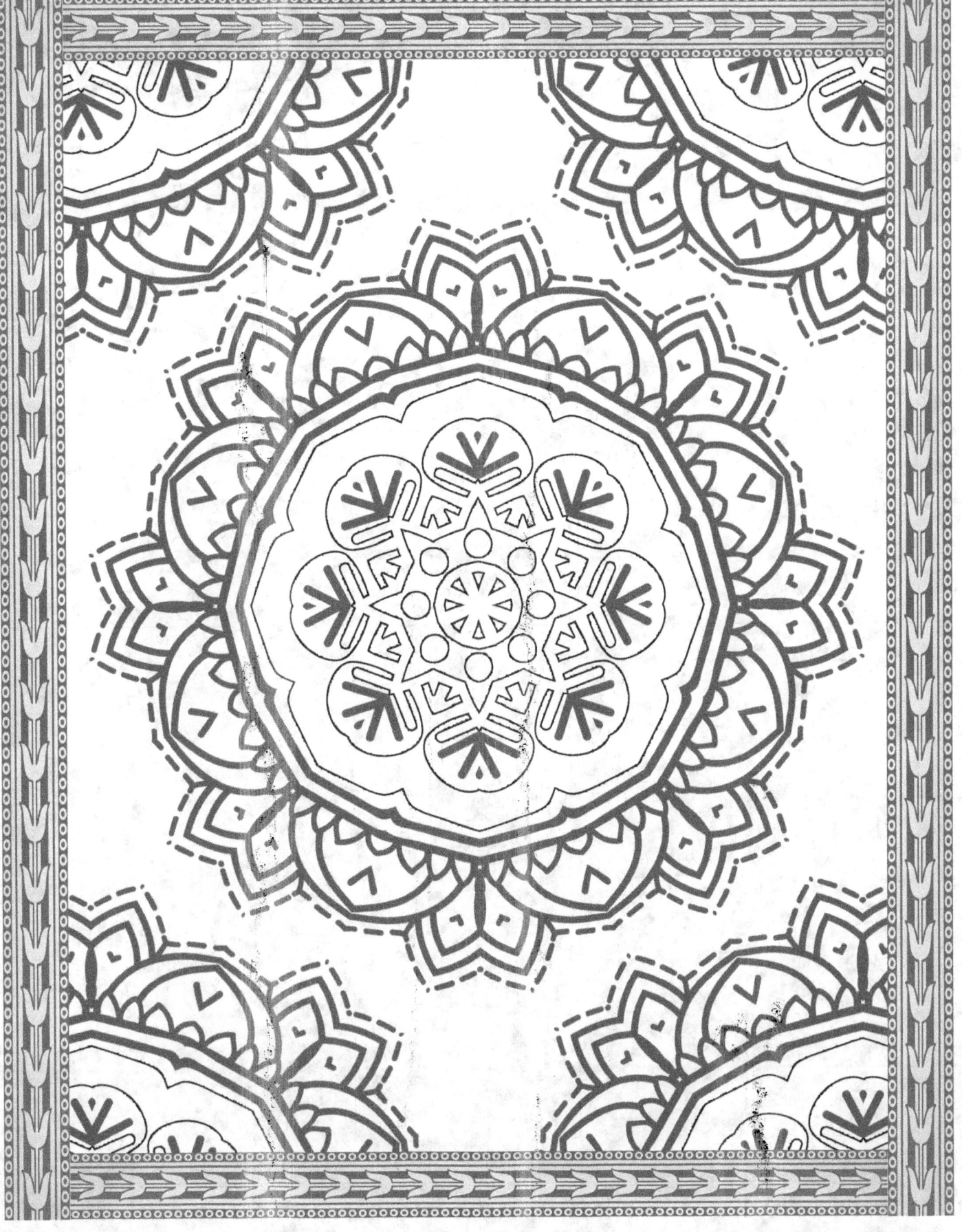

Dreams are symbolic in order
that they cannot be understood;
in order that the wish, which is the source
of the dream, may remain unknown

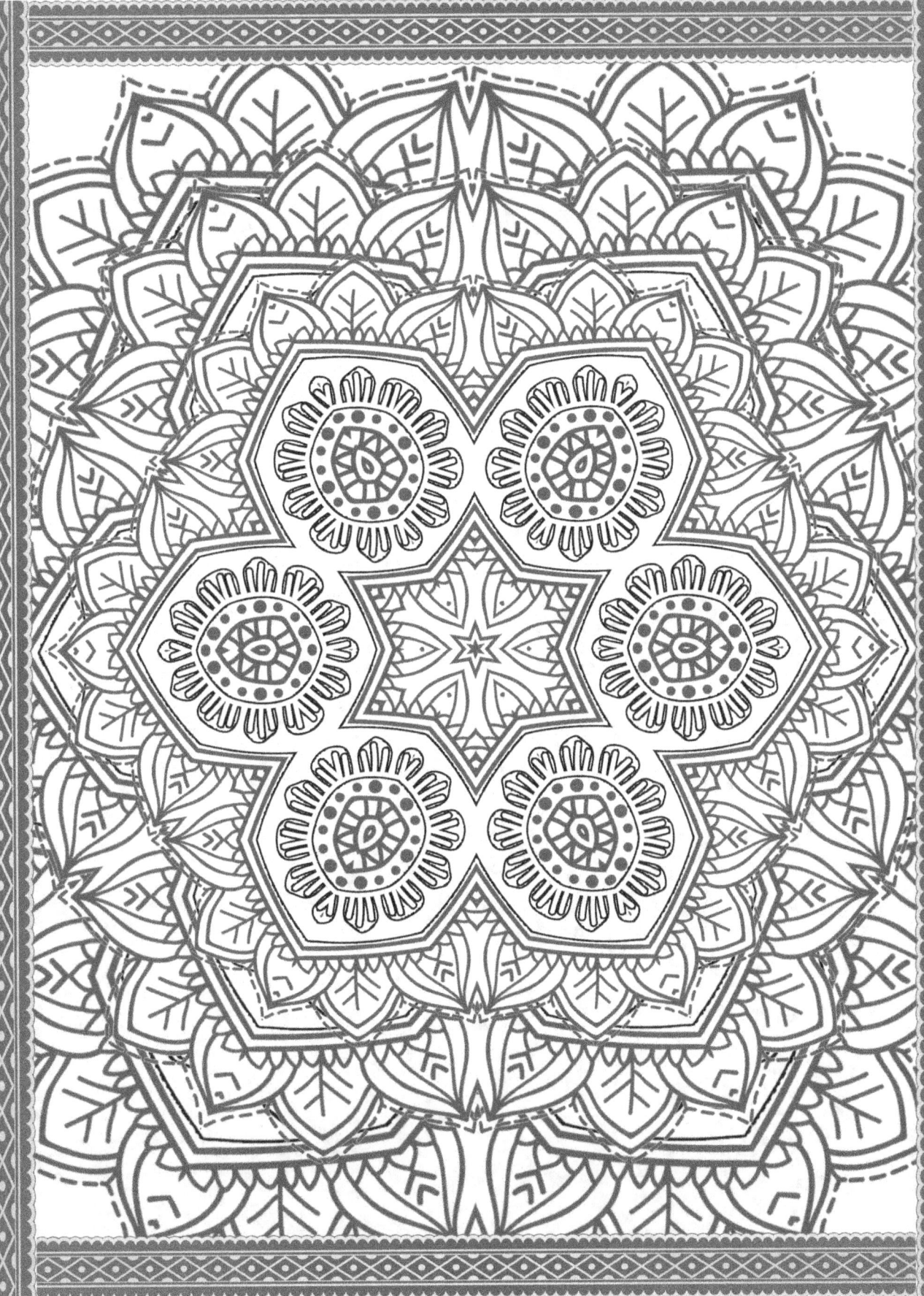

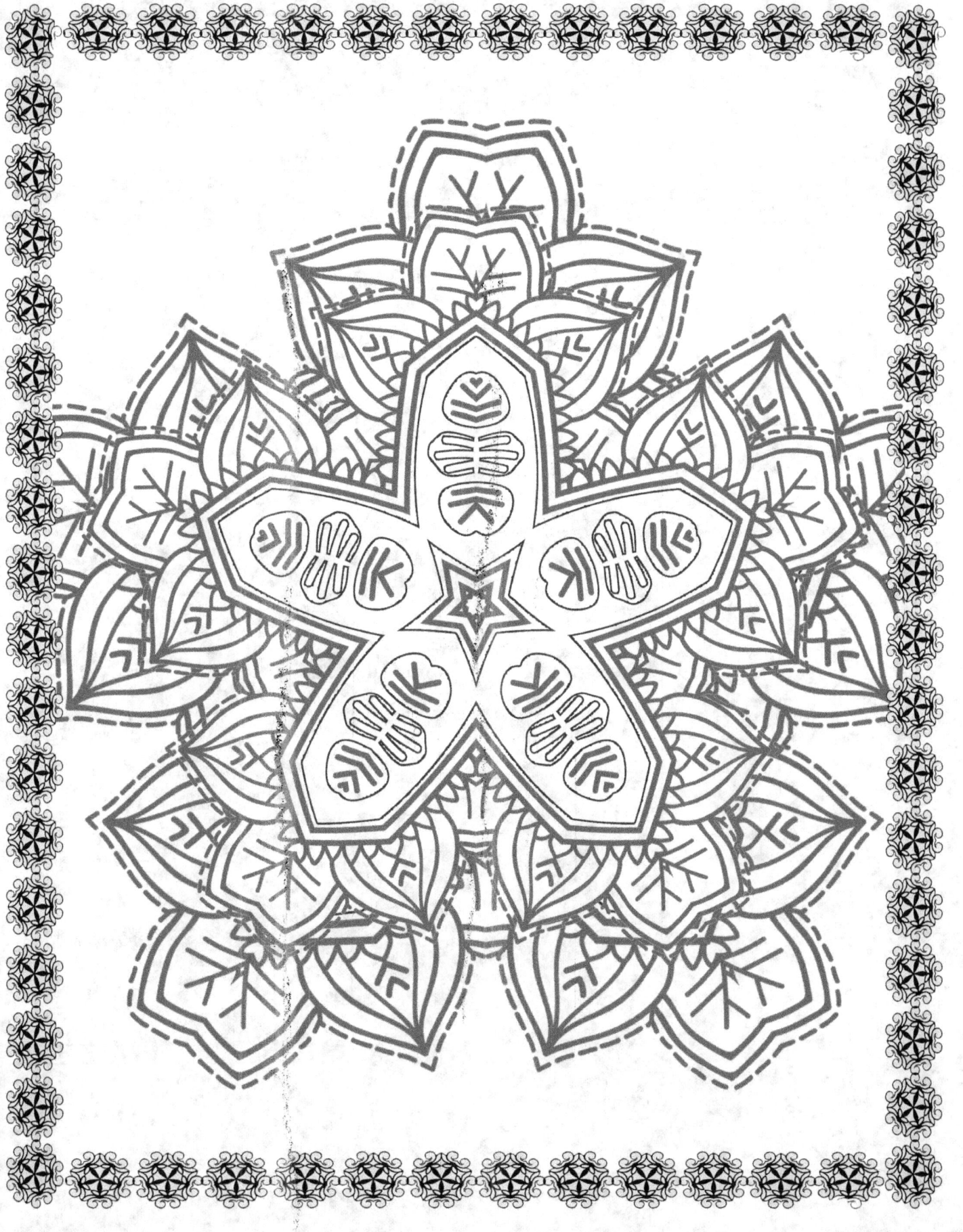

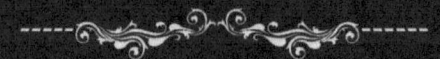

BETWEEN THE dreams OF night and day

there is not so great a difference

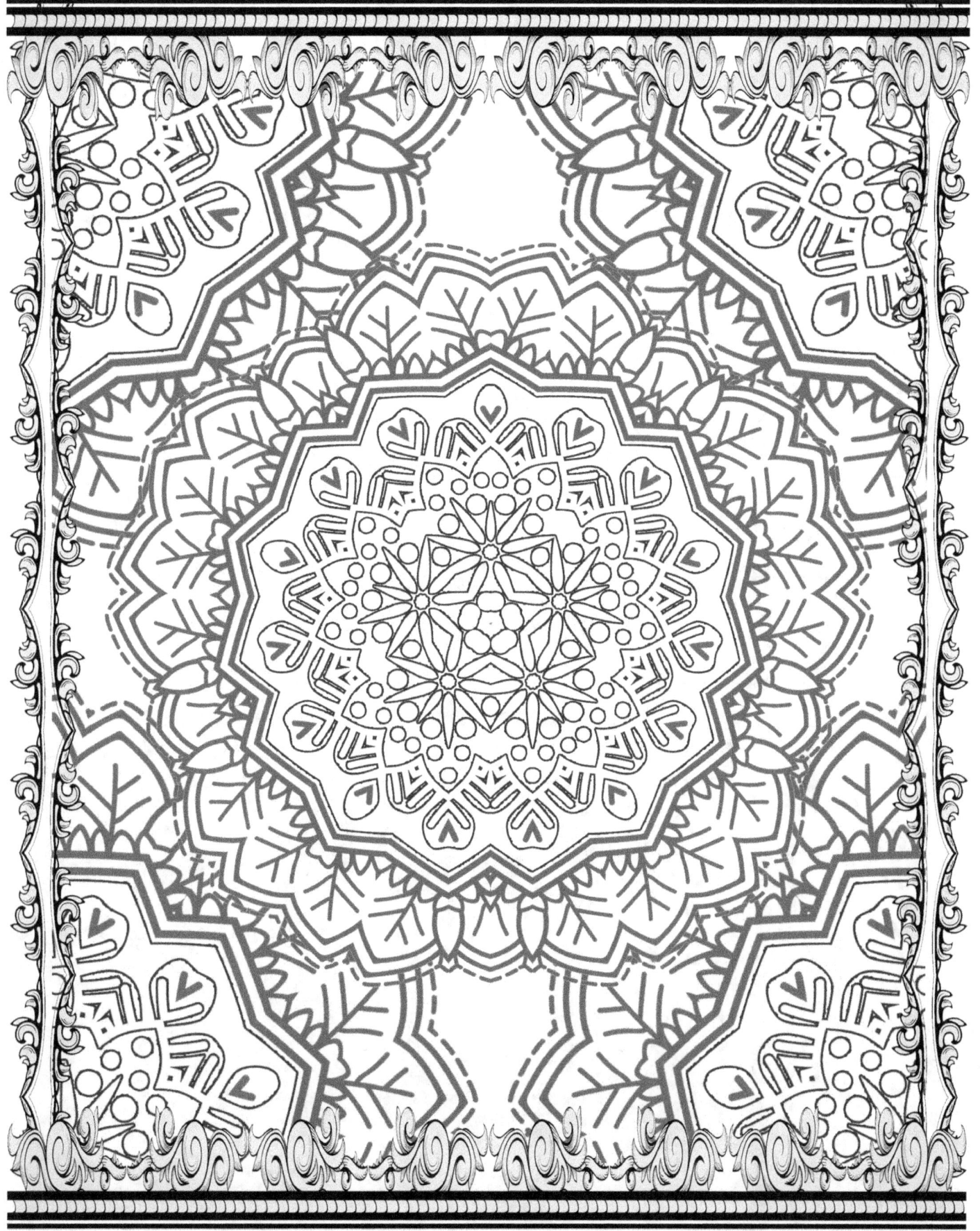

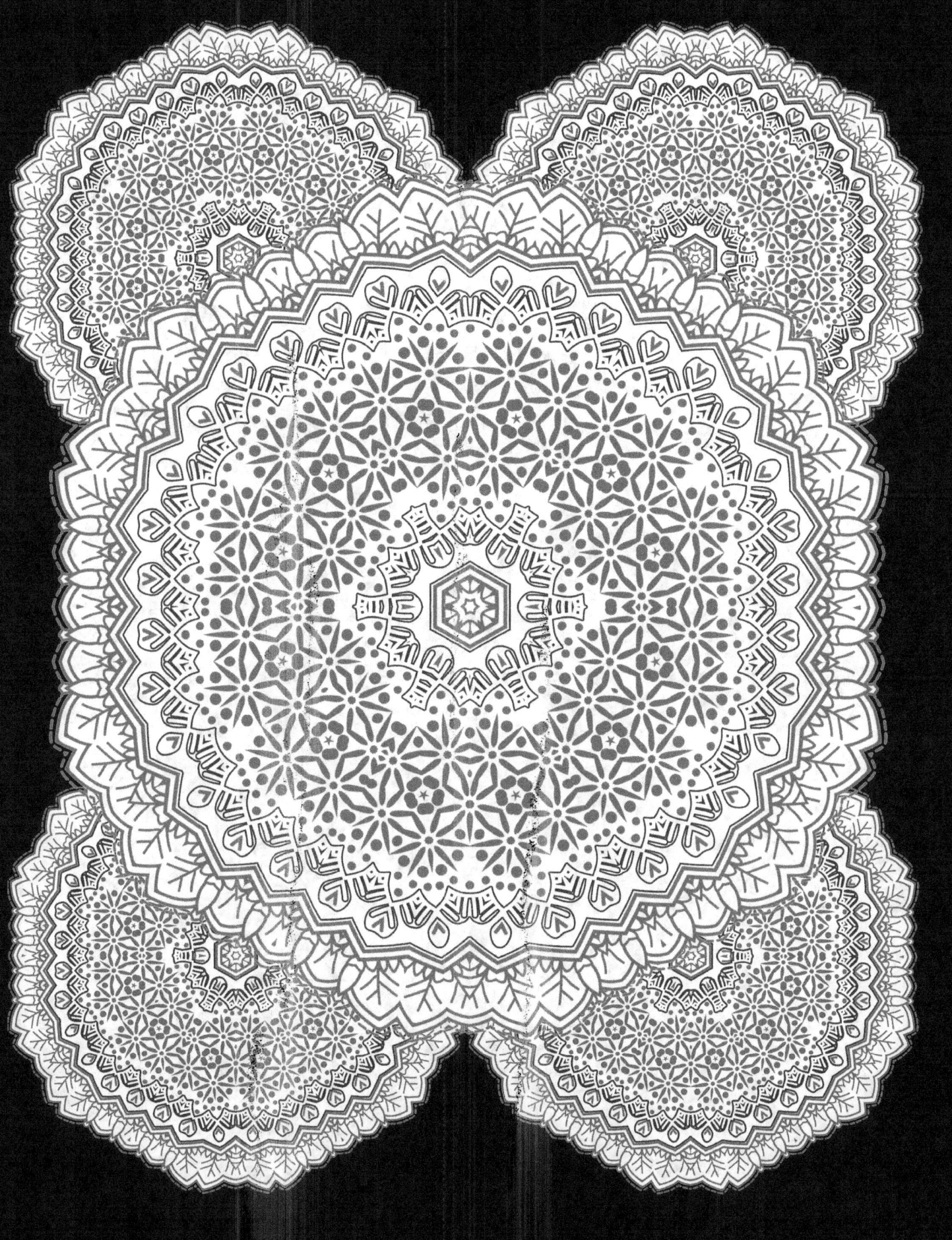

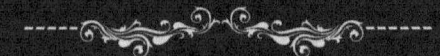

Nobody, as long as he moves about among
the chaotic currents of life, is without trouble

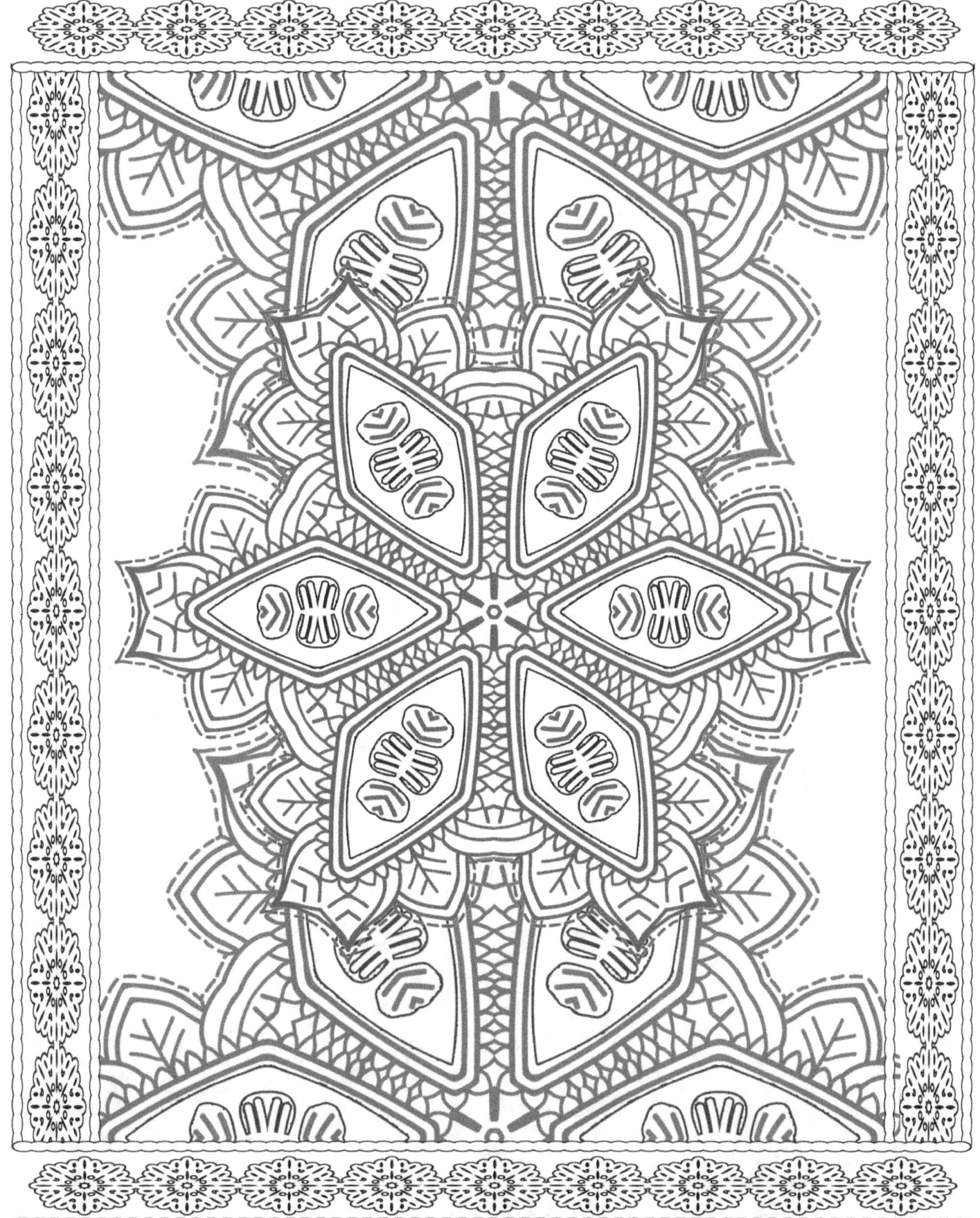

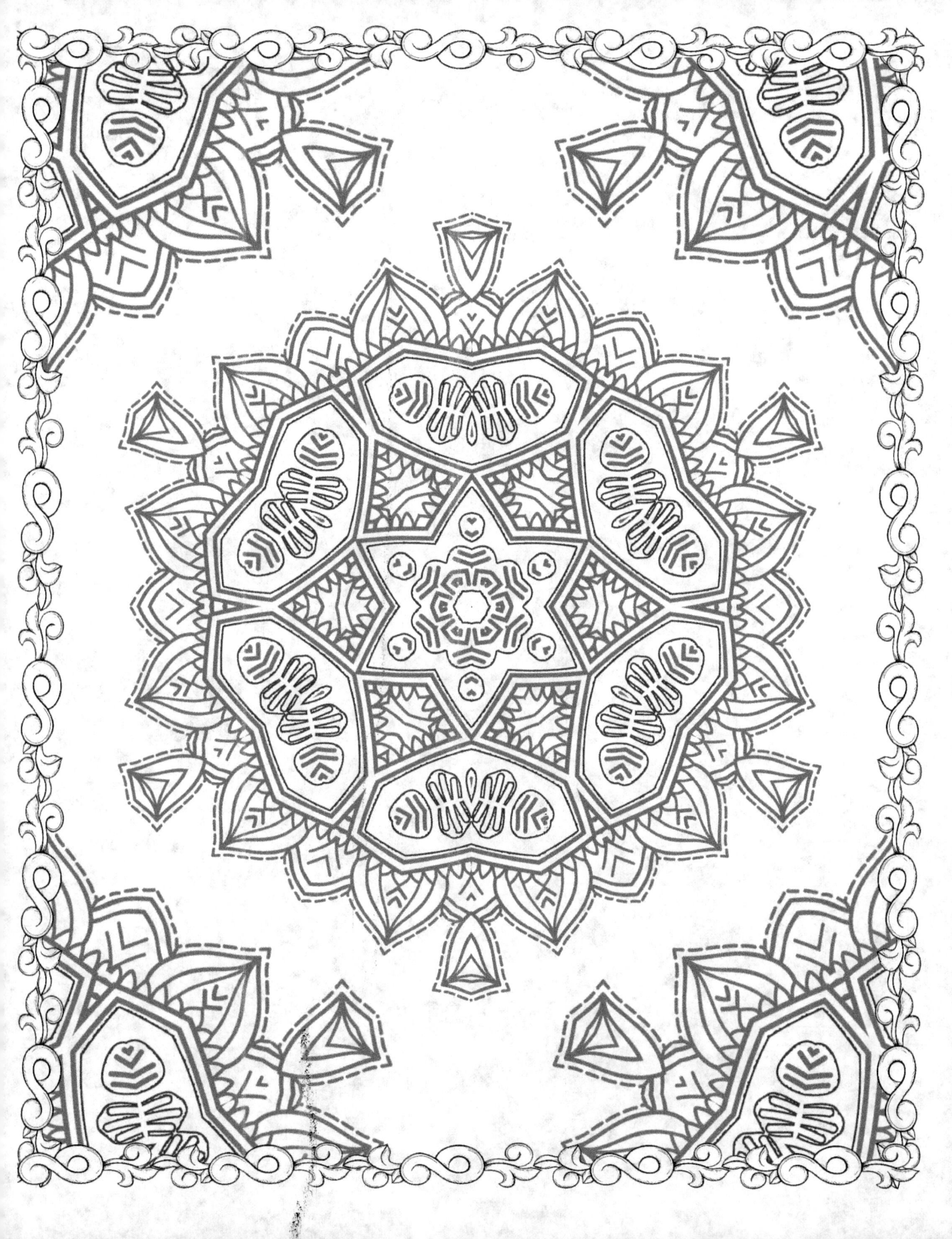

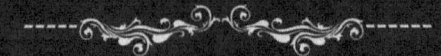

SYNCHRONICITY IS AN EVER PRESENT REALITY

FOR THOSE WHO HAVE EYES TO SEE...

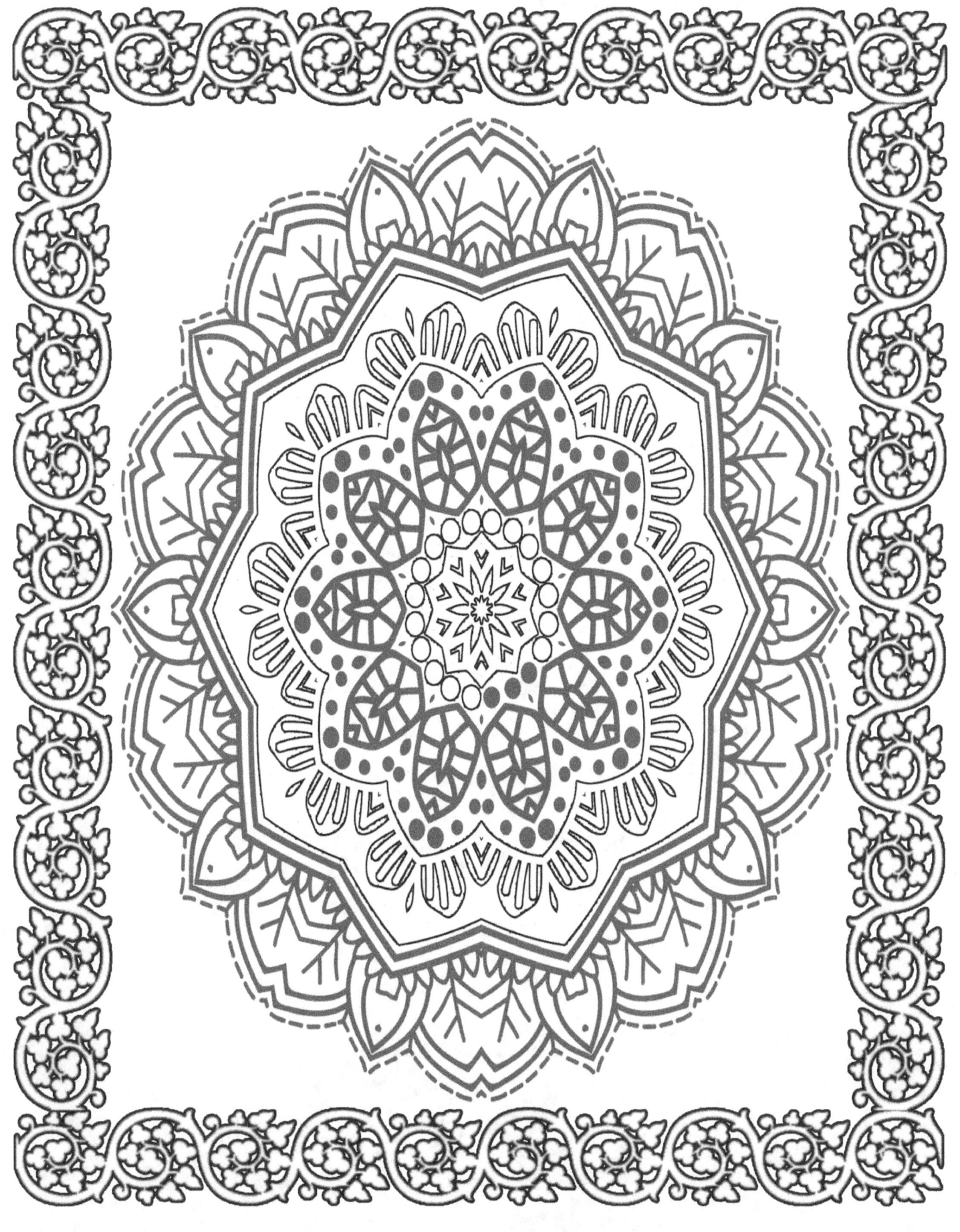

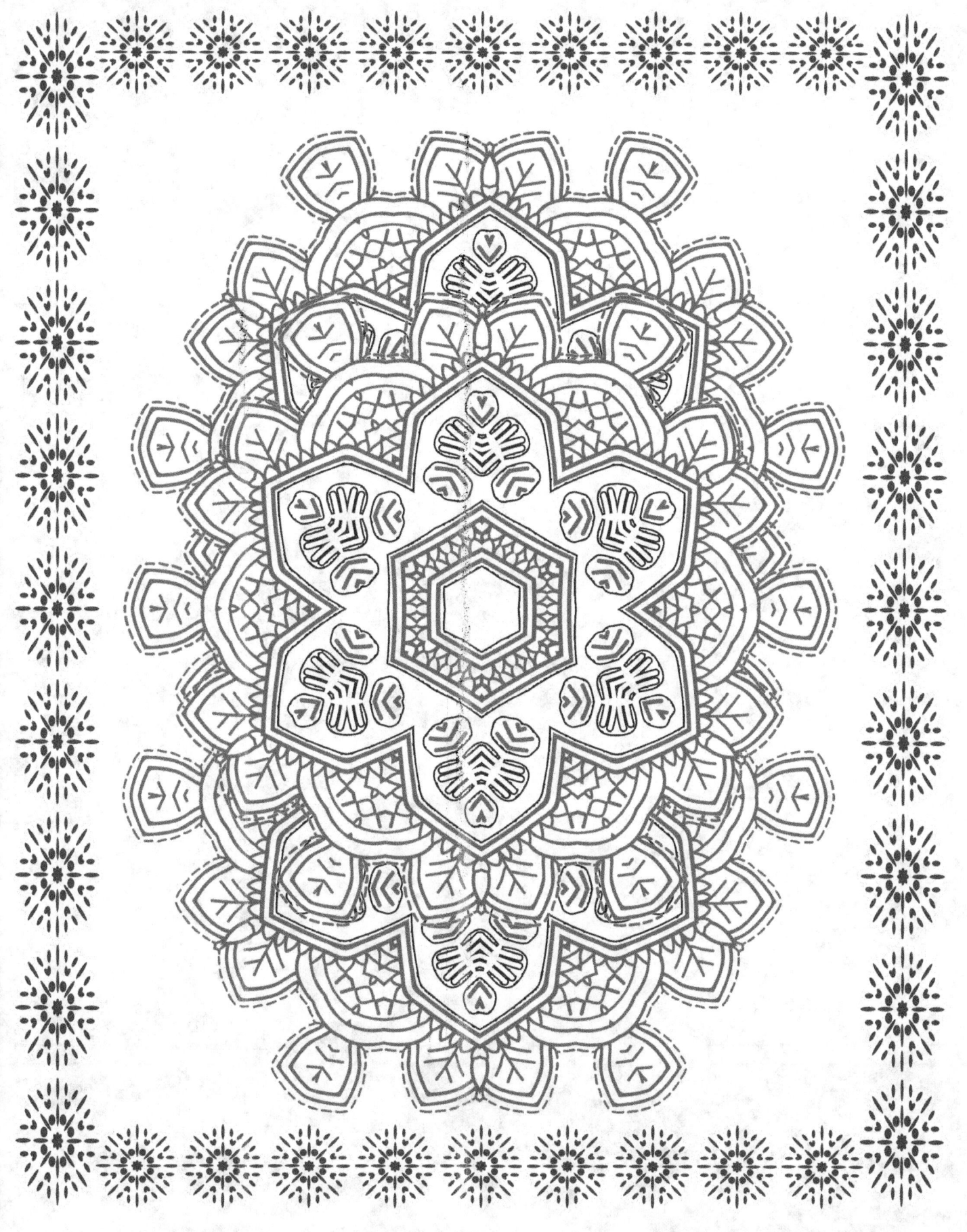

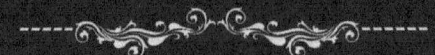

there can be no transforming of darkness into light
and of apathy into movement without emotion

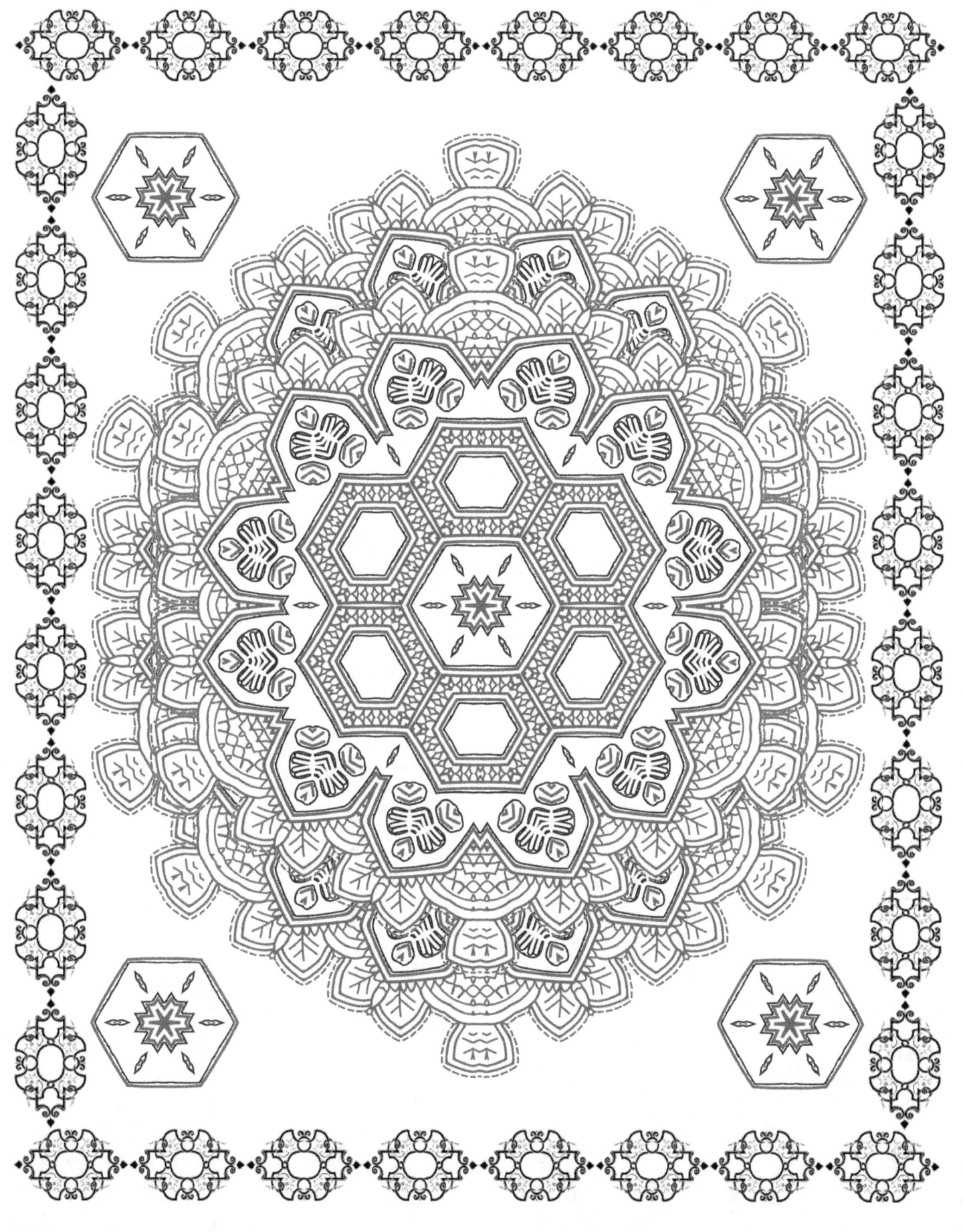

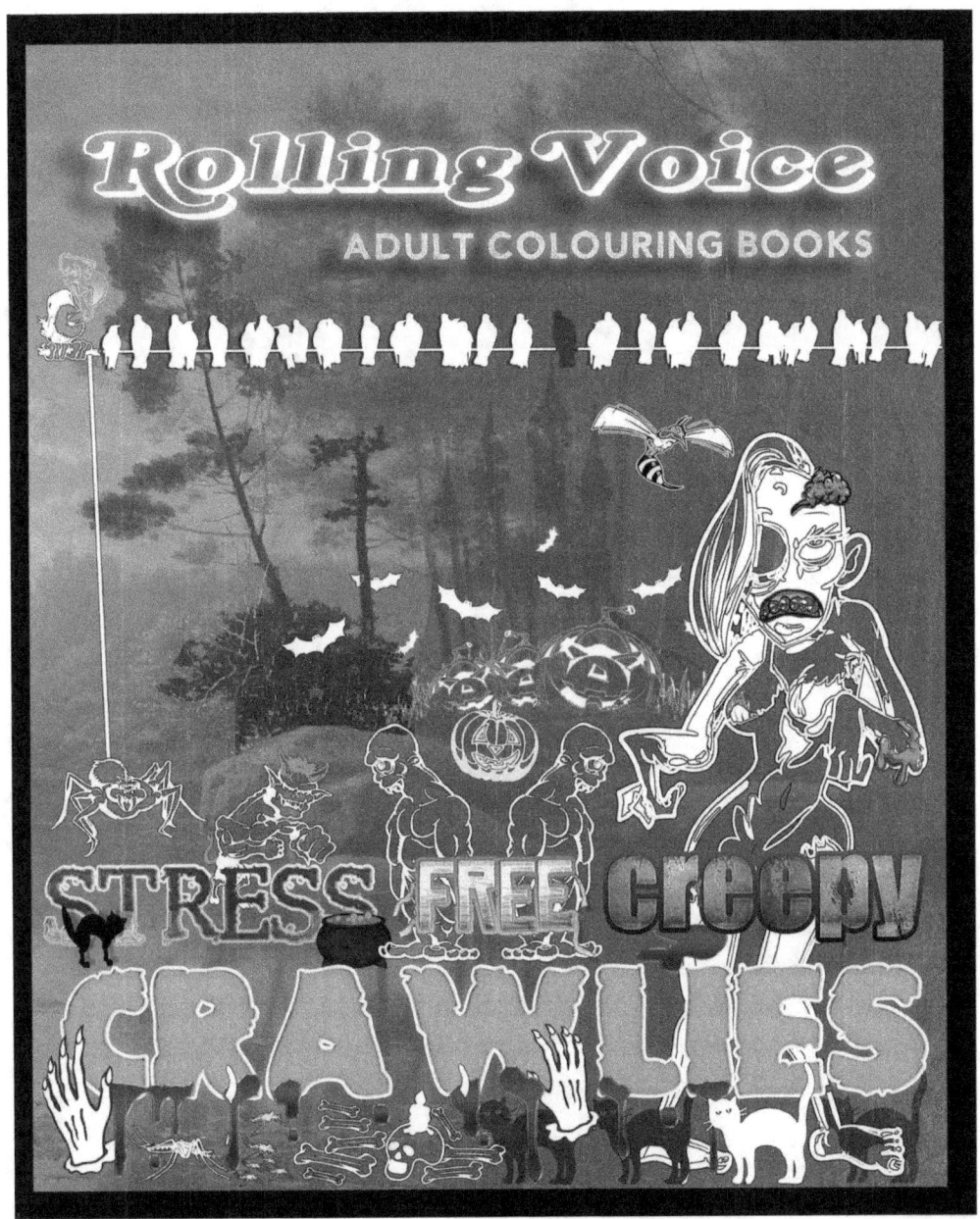

http://goo.gl/e5nKaZ
RollingVoice.com

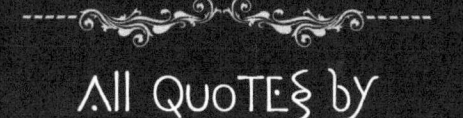

All Quotes by
Carl Gustav Jung
26 July 1875 – 6 June 1961

www.ingramcontent.com/pod-product-compliance
Lightning Source LLC
Chambersburg PA
CBHW081453170526
45166CB00008B/2409